D0286740

Passage
through the
Wilderness

Other Books by Zeb Bradford Long

The Collapse of the Brass Heaven: Rebuilding Our World-view to Embrace the Power of God (co-authored with Douglas McMurry)
Receiving the Power: Preparing the Way for the Holy Spirit (co-authored with Douglas McMurry)

To Marion
memory and

Passage
through the
Wilderness
A Journey of the Soul

Zeb Bradford Long

Chosen Books

A Division of Baker Book House Co
Grand Rapids, Michigan 49516

© 1998 by Zeb Bradford Long

Published by Chosen Books
a division of Baker Book House Company
P.O. Box 6287, Grand Rapids, MI 49516-6287

Printed in the United States of America

All rights reserved. No part of this publication may be reproduced, stored in a retrieval system, or transmitted in any form or by any means—for example, electronic, photocopy, recording—without the prior written permission of the publisher. The only exception is brief quotations in printed reviews.

Library of Congress Cataloging-in-Publication Data

Long, Zeb Bradford.
   Passage through the wilderness / Zeb Bradford Long.
      p.   cm.
   Includes bibliographical references.
   ISBN 0-8007-9262-9 (pbk.)
     1. Spiritual life—Christianity. 2. Wilderness (Theology) 3. Holy spirit.
   4. Long, Zeb Bradford. I. Title.
   BV4501.2.L657   1998
   248.8'6—dc21   98-7584

Unless otherwise marked, Scripture is taken from the Revised Standard Version of the Bible, copyright 1946, 1952, 1971 by the Division of Christian Education of the National Council of the Churches of Christ in the USA. Used by permission.

Scripture marked NASB is taken from the NEW AMERICAN STANDARD BIBLE ®. Copyright © The Lockman Foundation 1960, 1962, 1963, 1968, 1971, 1972, 1973, 1975, 1977, 1995. Used by permission.

Scripture marked NIV is taken from the HOLY BIBLE, NEW INTERNATIONAL VERSION®. NIV®. Copyright © 1973, 1978, 1984 by International Bible Society. Used by permission of Zondervan Publishing House. All rights reserved.

Scripture marked KJV is taken from the King James Version of the Bible.

For current information about all releases from Baker Book House, visit our web site:
                          http://www.bakerbooks.com

To all those who walked with me through the wilderness and helped sustain me along the way. Especially Laura: in love and deepest appreciation.

The Spirit immediately drove him out into the wilderness. And he was in the wilderness forty days, tempted by Satan; and he was with the wild beasts; and the angels ministered to him.

Mark 1:12

Contents

Introduction
to This
Strange Book

In my spiritual journey I have passed through many times of dryness and testing. Some call this spiritual state "the wilderness." Others have called it the "dark night of the soul" or "the valley." There are many names, but they point to the same spiritual reality.

Up to the writing of this book, I have passed through three especially intense times of wilderness. The reflections offered here represent my own attempt to reflect, biblically and theologically, on these experiences.

I went through the first time of wilderness testing when I was a student at Davidson College from 1970 to 1974—the period in which I decided to follow Jesus Christ in the midst of other attractive options. The second period was from 1978 to 1980 when I served a small church in rural North Carolina. This was my transition point from following a traditional path of ministry in the local parish to answering a call to power ministry on the mission field. The final period was from 1986 to 1990. This wilderness took place in the middle of successful, effective missionary ministry in Taiwan, when I turned 36 and went through what I now recognize as a severe midlife crisis. This experience of wilderness facilitated and resulted in another drastic change in ministry. In addition I have undergone a number of less intense but equally significant wilderness testings.

Looking back now, I am thankful to have had these and other wilderness experiences, for although they nearly destroyed me, they were times of intense engagement with God, resulting in deep spiritual growth.

Do not look for a chronological ordering of events in the book. There is none. The organization of the book is based, rather, on the phases of the wilderness journey itself. I have drawn experiences from my own life and the lives of others to make vivid each of these phases.

My motive in writing is twofold. First, I hope to help others who are in a dry period in their spiritual journeys. Second, I write out of obedience to the leading of the Holy Spirit as a means of my own healing from the wilderness experience. Writing this book (it was published originally in Chinese) helped get me through the desert by giving me insight into what had happened to me. Now, as I revise this book, I am no longer in the wilderness. Some of my experiences and thoughts strike me as extreme. But I have left them in the book because wilderness is an extreme time. To exclude these experiences, or to revise them to be more acceptable and understandable to those not in the wilderness, would be to distort reality.

For those of you who are happy with your lives and are experiencing usefulness and fulfillment in ministry, this book is probably not for you. Set it aside until the bottom drops out of your ministry, your marriage fails, you face overwhelming temptation or you are tormented by the silence of God. Then you may find this book useful. It is an extreme book, written for times of extremity in our spiritual journeys.

One other aspect of this book requires both explanation as well as forgiveness: It is intensely personal. I feel vulnerable putting this story into print. My story is messy and not very flattering. I describe struggles with lust and anger, pitched battles with God and encounters with evil spirits. I have taken the risk of sharing my heart and personal experience because of a liberating discovery: Often the deepest, most personal battles in our lives are those most universal to the human experience. By sharing them, I have found, I do for others what I wish someone had done for me—break through the loneliness of the wilderness by sharing with me their personal struggles.

Throughout the book is the assumption of the working of the Holy Spirit. I freely use such terms as *filled with the Holy Spirit, the Holy Spirit upon, baptized with the Holy Spirit* and *the gifts of the Holy Spirit*. I know these terms are problematic for many readers, but I do not use them in the traditional Pentecostal or charismatic way, nor do I refer to a "second blessing" as a second work of grace, or suggest that one must speak in tongues as initial evidence. I am coming at this from a completely different understanding. I have laid out a framework for understanding these operations of the Holy Spirit in my two books co-authored with Douglas McMurry, *The Collapse of the Brass Heaven: Expanding Our Worldview to Embrace the Power of God* and *Receiving the Power: Preparing the Way for the Holy Spirit.*

It is my hope that this book will help you not only survive the wilderness, but be transformed by it to become a more effective, Holy Spirit–empowered servant of Jesus Christ.

Part *one*

The Nature of the Wilderness

Am I
in Spiritual
Wilderness?

What was wrong with me? The day before, life had been so full. Suddenly, where I had known peace and fulfillment, I felt a terrible restlessness.

I had accepted the call to serve a small country church in North Carolina, mostly because of the promise that my wife, Laura, and I would have the opportunity to develop a prayer community at a church camp not far away. We had held this vision ever since serving in Korea as missionaries. Now the vision was shattered—and so was I.

Every day since moving to the church, I had run up the hill behind the manse where I could see the foothills of the Blue Ridge Mountains. The mountain with the camp on it, owned by the denomination, stood like a clear beacon on which I rested my hopes. Every day I asked God to bring the vision to reality and give birth to a prayer community there.

For this to happen was a real possibility since those who had received the vision warmly were connected with the church and could make it happen. A prominent pastor supportive of the vision had promised that I would be given the opportunity to present the plans to the committee that was to decide the future of the camp.

One day, however, I received the news that the church had sold the land. Not only had I not been given the opportunity to present plans to the committee, but I had not even been notified of the meeting. And for lack of any other plan, the committee had simply sold the land to a private investor.

I was shattered, swirling with hurt, anger and confusion. As I climbed the hill to my daily prayer spot, I cried out to God. He spoke a message—not to my natural ear but to my whole being. Its meaning resonated within me.

My son, I have taken the land away because you were beginning to trust the vision rather than Me, the giver of the vision. The vision will have its fulfillment in My means and in My time. You must learn to follow Me and Me alone.

Disappointment over the sale of the land plunged me into a spiritual state I did not understand. I felt depressed, but this depression had an intensely spiritual quality. I experienced a soul-deep restlessness and began to struggle with God, with myself and with the devil. I started to deal with temptations as never before. Where was I headed? I had no idea.

As you pick up this book, you may be asking the same question about your own situation. Are you in the wilderness or just depressed? Have you simply faced one of life's normal disappointments or is this a gateway into the wilderness state? To help you begin to explore such a possibility, I list some of the symptoms that those in the wilderness have experienced.

Some Signs That You May Be in the Wilderness

Restlessness that seems to flow from the depths of your being
A sense of God's absence

Spiritual dryness—prayer becomes empty, the Bible no longer speaks and worship no longer lifts you into the presence of God

More intense battles with temptation

Deep resistance to doing God's revealed will

Loss of joy and purpose, even when you are experiencing fruitfulness in ministry

The unpleasant awareness that you are being led to face things in yourself that you do not want to face

Confusion about calling and purpose

Fruitlessness in life and ministry

The first step in discerning whether God is calling you into a wilderness stage of your spiritual growth is to ask Him in prayer, "God, where am I? What are You doing? Are You driving me into the wilderness, as You have driven many of Your faithful servants before me?"

There is no neat test to know whether you are in the wilderness. As you read the following pages, you may recognize the spiritual topography as similar to your own and conclude that, yes, indeed, you are in the wilderness. In the next chapters we will consider the nature of the wilderness and observe some of the many ways we may be led into this spiritual state.

From the beginning it is important to recognize that wilderness, as a spiritual environment, is often hidden behind other painful or difficult conditions of life. Depression, disappointments in relationships, losing one's job, midlife crisis and other traumatic events—all are part of the human condition. From them we may learn much, but they are not in themselves wilderness.

And do not let spiritual wilderness obscure your possible need for medical help. One person I know battled depression for several years, thinking it was a form of spiritual wilderness that she was required by obedience to Jesus Christ to endure. Finally she sought medical attention and, after medication and therapy for unresolved life issues, her depression has lifted.

Most of the time Christians do not move beyond these external circumstances into the condition of their souls. Nevertheless, it is important to consider the possibility that your situation may indeed be wilderness. For if it is, God may have special blessings for you that you may miss if you deal with your situation simply as depression, midlife crisis or "bad luck." Further, if it is wilderness, the normal treatments for life's crises will not work. Your treatment and healing will come about only through engagement in the realm of the Spirit.

Let's move on, then, to discuss why God may lead His children into the wilderness.

Questions for Reflection

1. Where are you in your spiritual life?
2. Review the list of characteristics of the wilderness. Do any of them describe your present situation?
3. In prayer, ask God to speak to you about who you are in His Kingdom and where you are in your relationship with both yourself and Jesus.
4. As preparation for reading this book, and to help you discern whether you are in spiritual wilderness, draw a flow chart of your life. On this chart mark any significant turning points in your spiritual journey. Mark the high and low points of your faith and experience.

The Purpose
of the
Wilderness

J In Christ there is peace, joy and happiness. All true. But the haunting words of one hymn point to a concurrent reality:

> They cast their nets in Galilee
> Just off the hills of brown;
> Such happy, simple fisherfolk
> Before the Lord came down.
>
> Contented, peaceful fishermen,
> Before they ever knew
> The peace of God that filled their hearts
> Brimful, and broke them, too.
>
> Young John, who trimmed the flapping sail,
> Homeless in Patmos died.
> Peter, who hauled the teeming net,
> Head-down was crucified.

The peace of God, it is no peace,
But strife closed in the sod.
Yet, brothers, pray for but one thing—
The marvelous peace of God.[1]

The "marvelous peace of God" that we have in Christ also includes struggle, darkness and crucifixion.

The world is familiar with a cheap form of Christianity—or, it may more charitably be said, an incomplete form. It is taught by many, especially those like myself who have discovered the gifts and power of the Holy Spirit. We have expounded on God's healing and on His power to overcome obstacles and solve life's problems. We have taught that Jesus is the resurrection and the life, and that His resurrection power, through the Holy Spirit, is available to us right now.

This is all true; I have experienced it.[2] But there is more. At the center of our faith is a cross. Before the glorious resurrection, there is a bloody crucifixion. Our faith must embrace both; otherwise it is only half-true. A faith that is only half-true is bound for disillusionment. Like a ship navigated by an incomplete chart, it is in danger of being lost on the open sea or wrecked on the rocks.

The Kingdom of God has come in Jesus Christ. The powers of the age to come are at work, but Jesus' Kingdom is manifested in a world still in bondage to sin. The Kingdom has come but is not yet fulfilled. We still live in the in-between time, in an era of new life but also of sickness, struggle, and death. People are healed, but many others are not. For some, burdens are lifted; for others, there is no victory, only crushing defeat. Let's also look within ourselves. If we are in Christ, we are new creations, yet our old, sinful selves remain, like smoldering embers ready to leap into flame at the first wind.[3]

In this in-between time, Jesus does empower us through His Holy Spirit; He blesses us and promises that "he who believes in me will also do the works that I do; and greater works than these will he do, because I go to the Father" (John 14:12). But

Jesus also says to us, "If any man would come after me, let him deny himself and take up his cross daily and follow me" (Luke 9:23). Jesus opens the doors of heaven to us, and at the same time sends us back into the world, with its suffering and death.

The Place of God's Discipline

Those whom God loves, He disciplines, and often the place in which we experience this terrifying love of God is in the wilderness. Especially those chosen and anointed for spiritual leadership will receive this discipline. Most of the great figures in Scripture passed through times of wilderness preparation before being able to undertake God's work.

Joseph was cast down to the bitter lot of slavery before being exalted to a rank second only to Pharaoh. Moses spent forty years herding sheep before being sent back to free his people. After liberation from slavery in Egypt, the Israelites wandered for forty years in the wilderness before entering the Promised Land. King David, Elijah and Jeremiah all served time in the wilderness.

In New Testament times as well, most of God's anointed servants were sent into the wilderness. Peter, for example, after his denial; John, while on Patmos; Paul, after his conversion; and most of all, God's own beloved Son, Jesus Christ.

The wilderness is a place of desperation, of being lost, of darkness. It is a place where we die again and again; where we stumble and feel we will never arise. It is the place where all our illusions of self-sufficiency and self-righteousness are stripped away, showing our naked, sinful selves. In the wilderness the veneer of meaning is stripped away. Here we fall into the abyss of chaos and beyond, into a deeper abyss of God's mysterious love. In the wilderness we meet the devil in a thousand forms who tempts and torments us. We meet ourselves as enemy and friend. We encounter God in a combat of opposing wills. We may, like Jacob before the dawn, wrestle with Him and be forever wounded.

23

In the midst of this struggle, the shutters obscuring the Presence may be torn away and we may meet God as wrathful Judge but also as redeeming Father who loves us outrageously.

A Place in the Realm of the Spirit

The wilderness is not a geographical place, although it may correspond to a particular locale. Rather, with its unique topography, it is a spiritual reality. The wilderness is a journey of the soul, resulting in transformation. It is a stage in the Christian's process of spiritual and personal growth.

My own journeys in the wilderness have been lonely. No one seemed to understand or know just where I was. Those around me observed my external surroundings, which may have looked luscious and green, but never guessed that in my spirit I was traversing a wasteland. No one understood my restlessness, struggle or despair. They offered nice words of comfort: "God loves you"; "All things work together for good for those who love the Lord"; "Be patient, just obey"; "Tell the devil to leave." To someone in the wilderness, this was meaningless talk that left me lonelier than ever.

I offer these reflections not so much as a map, for each person's wilderness is unique, but as a sort of travelogue of some of the spiritual realities we may encounter. I offer these reflections as a word of hope to those in the wilderness. The path of desolation you must now walk is lonely, but it has been well worn by many of God's servants who have gone before you. Take comfort in the examples of those who have walked through the fire and lived. There is real hope; it is found in God and in Him alone.

I also offer these reflections to warn of the dangers in the wilderness journey. Along the way there is real cause for fear, for things do not always come out all right. The wilderness path is littered with the bones of those who perished along the way.

God said to those who refused to follow Caleb and Joshua into the Promised Land, "As for you, your dead bodies shall fall

24

in this wilderness" (Numbers 14:32). Let these words sink into your heart and remind you that the wilderness struggle is real and its dangers real. The battle may be won, but it also may be lost. You may emerge a mature child of God and be anointed to become a spiritual leader. Or you may end up a broken person unable to share in the great work of the Kingdom of God.

From where you and I stand, the outcome is truly uncertain. Perhaps even for God there is an element of risk. His gracious plans may be thwarted for a season, or He may lose a chosen servant. I suspect He has lost many. He nearly lost me.

To be lost to God—what a terrifying thought! I am not speaking of losing our ultimate salvation; our election into Jesus Christ is unshakable. Rather, I refer to whether we will have a part in the great work of Kingdom-building on earth.

What are some of the gateways through which the Spirit of God may drive you and me into the wilderness?

Questions for Reflection

1. Look honestly at your Christian life. How much of your walk with Christ has been characterized by times of joy and peace?
2. When you committed your life to Jesus, did everything begin to go better or worse? How much of your life since then has been characterized by suffering, disappointment or spiritual warfare?
3. In the midst of these difficult times, have you been aware of a soul-deep peace running like a subterranean river?
4. In your journal, note the difficult times and ask God to show you their purpose.

3

The Spirit
immediately drove
him out into the
wilderness. And he
was in the wilderness
forty days, tempted
by Satan; and he was
with the wild beasts;
and the angels
ministered to him.
Mark 1:12–13

Gateways into the Wilderness

The entry into the wilderness often follows a time of special blessing. The people of Israel were led into the desert after extraordinary demonstrations of God's love and power. Jesus was driven into the wilderness for testing after His baptism by John and the empowerment of the Holy Spirit.

It has been my experience, too, that wilderness follows times of new empowerment and spiritual growth. With the granting of power or renewed effectiveness in ministry, it seems, there must follow a period in which we are refined so as to be able to use faithfully the new power we have received. There may follow a time of even greater power and effectiveness. Thus, the wilderness may represent preparation for, as well as transition to, new ministry and service. It was after being tempted by the devil in the desert for forty days that Jesus, with great power, began His mission. Peter, after denying Jesus, was raised up to comfort his brothers in the faith and to lead the infant Church.

At the same time, the wilderness experience may be God's way of driving us to the point of surrender. Where we despair of our talents, we give up on our own vision and are finally ready to receive God's power and vision. This is what happened to Moses. It took forty years in the wilderness to die to his own visions and abilities before he was empowered by God at the burning bush. Wilderness may follow, as well as precede, our receiving the power of the Holy Spirit.

One matter must be fixed firmly in our minds before we begin. Just as the Spirit of God drove Jesus into the wilderness, the same Spirit may drive us into the wilderness. Many situations may serve as the means to bring us into the wilderness, and many will be the means of our anguish, but it is God the Father almighty who has led us there. During our wilderness experiences, He is the ultimate source of our pain and suffering, and He is the only means of our healing.

I heard Dr. Al Winn preach a sermon at Second Presbyterian Church in Richmond, Virginia, in the mid-1970s in which he offered a telling story and quote from John Calvin. In the last days of Calvin's life, he suffered terribly from what must have been cancer of the intestines. As the sixteenth-century reformer lay dying, he was heard by Theodore Beza to cry in agony, "O Lord, Thy hand is heavy upon me. O Lord, Thy hand bruiseth me sore. But it is enough, O Lord, to know that it is Thy hand."

This is a strange consolation, but no other can truly sustain us in this path through the wilderness. It is God who leads us there, and it is God who will lead us through it and into the Promised Land.

How will God lead you into the wilderness? Spiritual wilderness is like natural wilderness; it may be entered from many directions. There are many paths into the wilderness—some sharply defined, some entered only by degrees. It may come through some overwhelming temptation, or it may arrive by a drastic change in one's circumstances, or it may be a slow process of finding oneself gradually alienated from friends and cut off from God.

For me one of the gateways into the wilderness—a terrible one!—has been the conflict of loves.

The Conflict between Greater and Lesser Loves

While in college I spent a summer in India. Part of the time I lived in an old British hill station called Moosoorie located in the foothills of the Himalayas. I camped alone in a small, rustic cabin on a high ridge. Below me the plains of India were spread out like a carpet. Behind me towered the snow-covered peaks of the Nepalese Himalayas.

I knew deep down I was called to the ministry, but I was resisting giving my life completely to the Lord. The last thing I wanted to be was a minister. It was hard enough just being a Christian! God's persistent calling haunted me, however, and in the awesome beauty of that Himalayan hideaway, suspended between the mountains and the plains, I wrestled with God.

The story of the struggle need not be told here. Let me say simply that I yielded. Surrender was sweet, for God filled my heart with peace and assurance. And at the end of my stay in India, I returned to college with the full certainty that seminary and then full-time Christian service lay ahead.

I expected the peace to continue, but my decision to follow Jesus had to be tested and tempered in the wilderness.

My gateway into the wilderness as a college student started innocently enough. How can becoming friends with a beautiful woman who is a Christian possibly be a problem? Our personalities and interests clicked immediately. Before long we were in love. There was magic about our relationship; everything shone with new life. Our spirits, it seemed, were united; I could feel her pain and joy, and she mine. Each day we were together sparkled with the brightness of spring. Jointly we led one of the campus prayer groups and the Lord worked through us. It was a beautiful love—a love we both felt could have come only from God.

The happy days passed quickly. Then, slowly, I began to feel uneasy. The relationship was good, yet I sensed it was not right. At last, with absolute horror, I realized that the Holy Spirit was whispering in a dozen ways, *No! You must give her up. You cannot love her like this. You must turn and follow Me.*

"God!" I shouted, "What do You mean? Why? Why?"

I ran away. I denied it. But with persistence and unmistakable clarity, God spoke. He murmured to me in a still, small voice. In the depth of night He communicated through dreams. He spoke through the Scriptures. He shouted at me through circumstances. Yet I did not accept it.

"Please," I prayed over and over, "give me some sign to prove this really is Your will."

But there was only silence, filled with the nagging sense that the answer was still no.

I knew the will of God, but it was contrary to my will. Indeed, it was contrary to all of me. To obey seemed like killing myself, as well as killing someone I loved deeply. I was being asked to give up someone warm, real, present and whom I loved, for a greater but more intangible love. It all seemed impossible, irrational, yet deep down I knew I had to obey or be left out of what God was trying to do in and through me. This clash of wills was my gateway into the wilderness.

Sometimes to obey is sweet, and to seek first the Kingdom of God a joy. At other times to obey means to be willing to let yourself be broken and put to death, with no assurance that you will ever be raised up. It is the call to this sort of self-killing obedience that may drive us, stumbling, into spiritual wilderness.

It is a test of wills, but deeper still it is a test of loves. Lesser love must surrender to greater love. God so tested Abraham:

"Take your son, your only son Isaac, whom you love, and go to the land of Moriah, and offer him there as a burnt offering upon one of the mountains of which I shall tell you."

Genesis 22:2

Abraham must have thought God was crazy. Isaac was not just a beloved son but the fulfillment of God's promise of descendants. It was a test of greater and lesser loves, and of obedience. From the awful moment when the future patriarch received this command until he raised the knife to kill his son, Abraham must have lived a struggle as of a thousand years. With each step up Mount Moriah, he must have died a little, but like a man in a nightmare, he was driven on in obedience.

We face decisions in our lives, too, that are symbolic of deeper decisions. Beneath these decisions lie the diverging paths of our destiny and calling. What if Abraham had said to God, "No! You gave me my son. I have a right to keep him." We are left in suspense, for the Bible does not tell us. The text records only that God said, "By your descendants shall all the nations of the earth bless themselves, because you have obeyed my voice" (Genesis 22:18).

Truly, by obedience we will be blessed. But in the midst of the wilderness, we cannot know this. We experience only the struggle of deciding and the pain of dying.

Midlife Crisis: An Invitation into the Wilderness

Twenty years after my college experience, I walked through another gateway into a time of wilderness. I awoke one bright spring morning and discovered restlessness in my soul that had not been there the night before. When I listened to myself over the next weeks and months (which I tried not to do), I was frightened to find this discontent all-pervasive. I was restless with my work, my life, my marriage, my calling, my faith— everything.

I was 37 and loved my work. I knew I was in the right place. I was the director of a lay training center, which enjoyed effective ministry, and vice president of a college that was growing. I had a beautiful wife, a happy marriage, two lovely daughters and many good friends. Yet there it was—this strange restlessness, and beyond it, a gnawing sense of meaninglessness.

The words of Ecclesiastes became my own and articulated the condition of my heart:

> "Meaningless! Meaningless!" says the Teacher. "Utterly meaningless! Everything is meaningless."
>
> Ecclesiastes 1:2, NIV

One morning, for example, I was preaching to a packed sanctuary in a large church. Suddenly I was assailed with that sense of meaninglessness. So what if I was vice president of the college? So what if I could preach? So what if people came to Christ? In a hundred years nothing would matter. So what if I had a beautiful wife who loved me? In a hundred years she would be dead and so would I.

I kept on preaching, of course. I doubt anyone could tell I had a problem. But all these thoughts came like a gray cloud that hung over me and left a sick, empty feeling in the pit of my stomach. The only consolation I could find was back in Ecclesiastes:

> I denied myself nothing my eyes desired; I refused my heart no pleasure. My heart took delight in all my work, and this was the reward for all my labor. Yet when I surveyed all that my hands had done and what I had toiled to achieve, everything was meaningless, a chasing after the wind; nothing was gained under the sun.
>
> Ecclesiastes 2:10–11, NIV

Yes, that was exactly what I felt. King Solomon must have been a man just like me suffering a midlife crisis. Previously I had ridiculed "midlife crisis" as a bogus excuse for having an affair, getting a fast car or changing jobs. Then I found a major emotional and spiritual transition actually taking place inside of me.

In midlife crisis the armor of our natural strength and vitality begins to be worn away. We catch glimpses of our core being and realize with a shudder that there is no eternity in our hearts, only our own wretched mortality. During this period I saw sobering reminders everywhere that I would not live forever. I was tormented with the certainty of my own death.

I found myself haunted by something that had taken place a number of years before, while I served my first church. An old friend, Harris Ricks, and I had been walking and talking in a large, historic cemetery in Winston-Salem. As Harris and I were caught up in our favorite topic—what we planned to accomplish for God and the Church—we were not paying attention to the gravestones. Suddenly we turned a corner and came face to face with a large monument inscribed in bold but moss-eaten letters *Harris*.

We both stopped and I said, "Look, Harris, there you are!"

Harris looked at me with a smile. "Yes, there I am, but I suspect you're here, too. We're all here."

I laughed but was brought up short as we turned the next shrub-lined bend and I came face to face with my own grave marker. It was even bigger then Harris' and older. The chiseled letters, much worn by the weather, read *Long*.

We walked in silence for a long time.

In midlife crisis the terrible realization comes that someday, sometime you will die, and all your dreams, labor, money, accomplishments and relationships will be blown away to nothingness. I clung to Jesus' words to Martha:

> "I am the resurrection and the life. He who believes in me will live, even though he dies; and whoever lives and believes in me will never die. Do you believe this?"
>
> John 11:25–26, NIV

In my heart I wanted to believe, but with my whole body I did not feel this could possibly be true.

My response as a man (I do not dare to fathom what it would be like for a woman!) was to flee the fact of my own death and to grasp at life.

About this time I received a letter from a good friend suggesting that we buy motorcycles, quit our jobs, leave our families, bike through Burma and India and see if we could make it up to the Himalayas. It sounded to me like a really good idea, so I knew I was undergoing some kind of change and was in real trouble.

Other changes started taking place inside of me, too. In addition to the sense of meaninglessness I had about the work I was doing (it seemed empty and useless), I grew tired of being a missionary and tired of being a Christian. I was tired of being responsible. The little imperfections of life—especially in myself, my wife, my children and my work—became gigantic and intolerable. And the moral structures of right and wrong that had held firm most of my life started to crumble in the onslaught of sexual lust and a lust for power and intensity of life. I was frightened at what was happening.

Personalities are different, so the symptoms you face may be different from mine. Just know that your unique personality and situation will, if you face the onslaught of midlife crisis, provide you with your own unique hell.

I am now convinced, through speaking to many other men and through reading Ecclesiastes, that midlife crisis is a natural transition that takes place generally between the ages of 35 and 45. It is a time of incredible creativity but also of great danger. Midlife crisis becomes a gateway into the wilderness when the Holy Spirit uses this soul-deep restlessness to call you and me into engagement with ourselves, with the devil and with God. This engagement begins when we do not flee our mortality, but rather face it. By passing through this hell, we may come to the experiential appropriation of the true source of our life, Jesus Christ.

When you find yourself invited to pass through this gateway into the wilderness, what should you do? I offer the following hard advice born of having walked this path.

First, *chain yourself to the Word of God and to His law.* In the wilderness ahead you may not know right from wrong.

Second, *keep your focus on where the struggle and solution are.* It is always an inward battle of your soul in which you fight

33

with yourself, with the devil and with God. You must at all cost resist the temptation to think that if you just change your outward circumstances by getting a new job, taking up a new sport, having an affair or joining the Foreign Legion, you will quiet the internal restlessness.

Finally, *submit yourself to a wise friend who will hold you brutally accountable to God's Word and to His call on your life.*

Without these three anchors, you may well be swept away by the inner, raging currents that mark this creative but perilous period of transition.

Many Gateways into the One Reality

There are many gateways into the wilderness; the conflict of loves and midlife crisis are but two. Other gateways may be the death of some vision or ideal that has given your life purpose and direction (such as when my vision of the prayer community died). Or your parent or spouse may die, hurtling you into the void of loneliness. A door may close. A job may end. Sickness may lay waste to your body, and to your hopes as well. Even an unsuspected lump discovered in a routine checkup that proves benign may hurl you into the wilderness as you are forced to face your own mortality. A child may be born retarded. A marriage may crash in divorce, after which, in broken loneliness, you find the gateway into the wilderness. It may be your own sin and disobedience that opens the door, or it may be someone else's sin.

All these circumstances and more may be the gateways through which the Spirit of God drives you into the wilderness. There are some Christians who have not passed through the wilderness, but the spiritual journeys of most of us take us through such times. The terrain you face will be peculiar to your own situation and your own spiritual needs.

What is the wilderness like? How do we know when we are there? The silence of God and the absence of His felt presence are two marks of the wilderness. To these we turn.

Questions for Reflection

1. Ponder the decisions you are facing presently in your life. Look beyond the surface. Are they symbolic of deeper, more important decisions?
2. What, in the light of God's revealed intentions for human life, are the long-term consequences of these decisions?
3. What or whom do you love the most? Be honest.
4. Are you in midlife crisis?
5. How may God be driving you into the wilderness? Identify your present or past gateway.

The Silence of God

How marvelous it was when I first awakened to the presence of the Holy Spirit![1] The Scriptures burst into life. They became the living Word of God, speaking to me, serving as light for the path ahead and as bread for my soul. Through little nudges, God seemed to lead me each day. When I was obedient and followed these leadings, I was amazed at the results. As I prayed for others, images or words of Scripture came to mind, which when I spoke them out seemed to minister deeply to the other person.

Praise felt as natural as breathing. I found a freedom of expression that comes from the intimacy of being in the presence of God. There were also miracles. I saw people healed. God worked to change circumstances. In the gift of tongues I found a miracle in my own mouth! Best of all for me were the feelings. I experienced joy overflowing, excitement, peace like a river and a sense that God was powerful and could do all things. While I was on this mountaintop, my motto was, "Expect great things from God and attempt great things for God."[2]

Then I arrived in the wilderness.

All that I had experienced was very real, for it is part of walking with the Holy Spirit. But there is another part of walking with the Spirit that is equally real—the times of the silence and apparent absence of God in the wilderness.

God, where are You? I prayed. *Why don't You do something?* Silence.

God, please speak. Give me some evidence that You are real, that You care, that You love me.

There was no evidence, only emptiness.

God, which way do I go? Which way is Your will?

No answer.

O Lord, it used to be that fellowship with You was sweet and I experienced Your presence every day. You were so real. Now I feel nothing.

In times like this we are left feeling abandoned, reaching out into nothingness, speaking words to a God who has apparently ceased to exist. That we could ever have rejoiced in His presence or experienced His power now seems a delusion.

The silence of God often takes place in the context of broken relationships, a lack of communion and community with others. In our noisy world we sometimes need silence; but if outward stillness resonates with the inward stillness of the absence of God, then silence becomes terrifying.

The silence of God that marks the wilderness takes different forms and has many causes. Let's look at three of them.

Silence Caused by Sin

After the death of Samuel, King Saul was tormented by a wilderness of the silence of God. He did not pass through it alive. Faced with the approaching army of the Philistines, Saul sought God's guidance desperately but was met only with silence. "When Saul inquired of the LORD, the LORD did not answer him, either by dreams, or by Urim, or by prophets" (1 Samuel 28:6). So devastating was this silence of God, and so desperate was Saul for guidance, that he sought out a spirit medium who could call up the spirit of Samuel. When Samuel appeared and spoke the word of God, it was a word of judgment. Saul and his sons would be killed, his army defeated and the kingdom given to David. God's silence, by "tempting" Saul to disobedience, drove Saul to his own destruction.

Saul experienced the silence of God because of his sin. Sin, in all its forms, cuts us off from the presence of God and dulls our hearing. The problem is not with God's hearing, but with our sin blocking communication:

> Behold, the LORD's hand is not shortened, that it cannot save, or his ear dull, that it cannot hear; but your iniquities have made a separation between you and your God, and your sins have hid his face from you so that he does not hear.
>
> Isaiah 59:1–2

The wilderness, when silent and devoid of God's presence, should drive us to our knees and compel us to search our hearts for sin. Only true confession and repentance may unstop our spiritual ears and restore to us our Creator's presence.

We must also know that if, during a time when God does not speak, we turn from Him and seek other means of communication with the spirit realm, we will only drive ourselves further into the darkness. The New Age movement offers a plethora of means, from channeling to meditation, for communicating with the natural and supernatural worlds. But God, who intends that our ears be for Him and Him alone, forbids all these to the Christian. They are forbidden because they really do work. Through these means we actually can contact the spiritual realm. But because they are outside of God's protection, they are gateways into deception and oppression by evil spirits.

The silence, however, is terrible, and feels in the core of our beings like a void or abyss. Our temptation is to flee this emptiness and seek consolation in drugs, gambling, adultery or even in good things like hard work and love of family. That, too, is the way into the deeper silence of spiritual death.

In times like these, we must cling like drowning men to our disciplines of prayer and devotion. For although prayer may

have lost its sweetness and our devotion become an empty ritual, these represent the only way out. We must also, with brutal determination, seek to be obedient to all we know of God's
will. This is our only defense against falling more deeply into
sin. Perhaps before our own strength fails and we, like Saul, fall
to our destruction, God in an act of undeserved mercy will
restore us to His presence.

Was Saul utterly lost? Was he damned? Will we be if we follow his path? These questions are for God to answer, not us.
It is certain, however, that God discarded Saul from a role in
the protection of Israel. Because of Saul's disobedience, the
Spirit of God left him and rested on David. In the same way,
we, too, may lose the anointing of the Holy Spirit and be left
out of the flow of God's purposes.

After King David sinned with Bathsheba, surely he was
haunted by the memory of his predecessor, Saul, losing God's
Spirit. David cried out to God with this prayer:

> Have mercy on me, O God, according to your unfailing love;
> according to your great compassion blot out my transgressions.
> Wash away all my iniquity and cleanse me from my sin. . . . Cre-
> ate in me a pure heart, O God, and renew a steadfast spirit within
> me. Do not cast me from your presence or take your Holy Spirit
> from me. Restore to me the joy of your salvation and grant me
> a willing spirit, to sustain me.
>
> Psalm 51:1–2, 10–12, NIV

Though our sin may differ from King David's, his prayer of
confession may become ours. If it is sin silence that you face,
David's prayer is the only way back to the presence of God.

The Silence of a Hard Obedience

Another form of the silence of God comes when we have
already received guidance. We know in our hearts and through
Scripture what God's will is for us and we have arrived at a
crossroads. We know which road to take, but it is the more dif-

39

ficult way. So we reach out to God, asking for some sign, some consolation to make it easier, but none is given.

Jesus knew in His heart and announced to His disciples that He must go to Jerusalem to be killed. He knew, too, that He would rise again from the dead (see Mark 9:31). This was the will and promise of His Father. Yet when the time came, Jesus struggled alone among the silent trees of Gethsemane. For human support and comfort He had taken His most beloved disciples with Him, but they abandoned Him and fell asleep. As He turned His eyes toward His Father, seeking solace, pleading that the cup be removed, He was met with silence and abandonment. His Father was unyielding as granite in His insistence that the way of obedience was the way of the cross. The only light Jesus received that night was that of the torches carried by the crowd coming to arrest Him.

Throughout the trial, and all the way to the crucifixion, God did not alter His will and intention. He did not intervene, nor did Jesus come down from the cross. In the heart of Jesus as well, God must not have broken His silence, for at last Jesus cried, "My God, my God, why hast thou forsaken me?" (Mark 15:34). He died rejected by humanity and abandoned by God.

Often in a long, hard obedience, we may feel abandoned by God. We may seek a sign or some special grace to make the obedience easier, but all we have and will likely ever have is a deep knowing that "Yes, this is God's call." We must decide, act and carry through as Jesus going to the cross, even though in our hearts we cry again and again, "My God, my God, why hast Thou forsaken me?"

When this is our case, we must continue along the road we know is right. If necessary, we must drive ourselves forward with the whip of the fear of God, while clinging to the hope that ahead must surely lie blessing and resurrection. Along the way God may surprise us with His grace and carry us awhile. He may lead us off the hard, dry road for a time of refreshment by some cool spring.

As I write this, it sounds reassuring, but in the pain of the moment we may lose all hope. Walking in the silence seems like an endless travail.

When There Is No Revelation, Go Fishing

> Simon Peter said to them, "I am going fishing." They said to him, "We will go with you." They went out and got into the boat; but that night they caught nothing.
>
> John 21:3

What are we to do when God does not speak clearly? Go fishing.

After Jesus was resurrected from the dead, He appeared to the disciples and presented to them His nail-scarred hands. As the Father had sent Him, He told them, so they were being sent. With this commissioning came the promise of the Holy Spirit (see John 20:21–23).

After this appearance, and before the promised outpouring of the Holy Spirit, the disciples entered an in-between wilderness time. The time of walking with Jesus in the flesh was over, but the time of Holy Spirit–empowered ministry had not yet come. Perhaps for the disciples, especially for Peter, this was also a time of personal turmoil and indecision. They had all forsaken their Master. Peter had denied Him three times, but the others had all run away, too. They had sinned and Jesus had not yet fully restored them. There seemed to be no clear guidance as to what to do next.

What to do? They used their own minds, fell back on their instincts and did what came naturally. Peter said, "I am going fishing," and the rest (apparently for the lack of anything else to do) followed.

Often God does give direct and clear guidance. At other times, however, everything in our minds and hearts is muddled and the will of God is obscured. We experience no clear calling, yet still we must decide and act. We must live in the world and be faithful to God there. So what do we do? Seek out wise counsel, search the Scriptures, understand our situations and then use our minds and hearts to make the best decision we can. We go fishing! We carry on, even though it may mean walking in the dark.

The disciples fished all night and caught nothing. Likewise, our work during those times may be fruitless.

Since we all like to be certain that we are in the will of God, these occasions of not knowing try our faith and our patience. I have found consolation in two things. First, for the disciples, it was while they were fishing that Jesus suddenly appeared to them. So it may be for us that, as we walk faithfully without clear assurance, Jesus breaks the silence and either gives us the guidance we need or else blesses our work. This He did with the disciples, as He commanded them to cast the net on the other side of the boat.

When God does finally give guidance, on the other hand, we may discover we were wrong and are now walking up a dead-end street. When this happens—and this is the second thing that consoles me—we trust God's love and forgiveness and know that our standing with Him rests not with our success but with His unmerited grace.

Much of the time following God is like fishing in the dark. This has especially been true for me during the wilderness periods.

When I returned to the United States to become executive director of Presbyterian and Reformed Renewal Ministries International, I entered a strange time similar to what the disciples must have lived through. I had received a clear calling from God to take up this work. Further, while spending six months in the mountains of North Carolina, I had been caught up in many moments of sweet intimacy with God in which He birthed in me a clear vision to guide the development of PRRMI's ministry. Then, right after Christmas 1989, Laura and I moved to Oklahoma City. That was stepping into the wilderness.

It was a time in which I saw no clear sign of God's presence and received no clear guidance as to what I should do. Yet before me lay dozens of decisions that I knew would set the future direction of the ministry. Further, God was not blessing the ministry financially, so Laura and I had to draw on our savings just to live. What to do?

I went fishing! I fell back on my own reason and started to work pragmatically to do the things that were consistent with the vision. Yet I did them without strong assurance from God that they were right. I also did them without seeing any fruit. I fished in the dark.

One brilliant, starlit night, Laura and I walked and prayed together. She was worried about our financial situation. Deep down I was beginning to think I had missed the leading of the Holy Spirit in accepting this call. As we talked, we laid our situation before God and told Him what He already knew. We could hold out, walking in the dark, using up our savings, for about a year. If after that time we still received no clear sign of His blessing, we would conclude that we had missed His will in accepting this call to PRRMI.

Still the silence persisted. I sank into a morass of details of administration. I did, however, go fishing as best I knew how.

One toss of the net was to call a team of pastors together to pray for guidance about how to equip people for Holy Spirit– empowered ministry. Out of this prayer time, the Dunamis Project was born. Richmond pastor Doug McMurry and I started writing the manual for the first event on the work of the Holy Spirit.

Then, in the winter of 1991, we offered our first event. Archer Torrey joined Doug McMurry and me on the teaching team. To my amazement 140 people showed up for the five-day event. On the last day of the retreat, the Holy Spirit was poured out on most of those present. As I watched the people being blessed, Jesus broke the silence and affirmed to me in my heart that the work was on track. What I was seeing was a first glimpse of what He planned on doing through PRRMI all over the world.

The Doctrine of Election: Hope while Fishing in the Night

In the wilderness of the silence of a long obedience, when we must fish in the dark, God gives us an extraordinary hope.

43

> Praise be to the God and Father of our Lord Jesus Christ, who has blessed us in the heavenly realms with every spiritual blessing in Christ. For he chose us in him before the creation of the world to be holy and blameless in his sight. In love he predestined us to be adopted as his sons through Jesus Christ, in accordance with his pleasure and will—to the praise of his glorious grace, which he has freely given us in the One he loves.
>
> Ephesians 1:3–6

Yes, this is the controversial and, most of the time, incomprehensible doctrine of election! I had not appreciated it until I was swept into the wilderness. There the promise that God, out of His love for me, had elected me into His Kingdom before the foundation of the world served as a great consolation.

Like the stabilizing keel of a sailboat, the knowledge that we are eternally elected sets us free to sail into the winds or into a storm, without fear of being swept away. We must decide, and the burden of our freedom may be more than we can bear. But at the same time we are free to decide, even if wrong, because we have the certainty that the fulfillment of God's purposes rests not with us, but with His sovereignty.

Let's fix these words of Paul in our hearts, then, as a support when we must fish through the night:

> We know that in everything God works for good with those who love him, who are called according to his purpose.
>
> Romans 8:28

The Silence of God's Presence

A third form of silence is God's presence with us.

> The LORD said, "Go out and stand on the mountain in the presence of the LORD, for the LORD is about to pass by." Then a great and powerful wind tore the mountains apart and shattered the rocks before the LORD, but the LORD was not in the wind. After the wind there was an earthquake, but the LORD was not

in the earthquake. After the earthquake came a fire, but the LORD was not in the fire. And after the fire came a gentle whisper.

1 Kings 19:11–12, NIV

Elijah was a colossal man of God. He moved in the power of God because he responded to His voice. He acted as God directed—and God always accomplishes what He directs.

Elijah challenged King Ahab and the whole apostate kingdom of Israel. He called for a three-year drought as the judgment of God on the kingdom. On Mount Carmel he challenged four hundred prophets of Baal to prove the existence of their god by calling down fire on the altar. They were unable to strike so much as a spark, proving the unreality of Baal. Then Elijah stepped forward, rebuilt the neglected altar of Yahweh and called down fire on the offering. After God's fire burned up the sacrifice, Elijah put to death the four hundred prophets of Baal, then prayed for rain. Shortly afterward, in mighty torrents, it fell. With the power of the LORD upon him, Elijah ran ahead of Ahab's chariot all the way to Jezreel.

Surely this prophet, who could at the word of the Lord call down fire and command the rain, would fear no one. But when Queen Jezebel vowed revenge for the deaths of the prophets of Baal, Elijah was terrified. He could do nothing but flee.

What had happened to him? Had he lost his faith? Had he lost his hearing? Did he no longer experience the anointing of Yahweh's Spirit upon him? Had the contest with Ahab exhausted him physically and spiritually? Was this burnout?

Whatever the reason, as Elijah cried out to God to take his life, he seemed a diminished man who had forgotten the mighty acts God had performed through his hands. In order to make him useful again, God had to drive His servant Elijah into the wilderness, back to the mountain of the Lord. There, in the silence of the wilderness, Elijah could again hear God's still, small voice. And with his return of hearing came a return of his power and mission.

The return to God's silence is something Jesus needed to do as well. Many times the Messiah left the crowds and noise of His ministry and went apart with His disciples or to a lonely place to pray. In the silence of the wilderness, He could communicate with God and keep His hearing keen. Usually He retreated like this either before or after times of intensive ministry (see Mark 1:12, 35; 3:7–13; 6:30–32; 9:2–8; 14:32–42; Luke 22:39–46).

Like Elijah and Jesus, contemporary servants of the Lord may become so active, with their lives so full of noise, that they can no longer hear God's still, small voice. When this begins to happen, their power and effectiveness wane. Then God sometimes drives His servants back into the wilderness for a time of silence. There they may experience His presence anew and find their hearing restored.

If we are to remain effective in ministry and service, we must let God lead us from time to time into the silence of the wilderness. We may go voluntarily by taking a retreat, or we may be driven there by circumstances. Generally it is less painful if we awaken to our need and seek silence ourselves. In this kind of wilderness, the silence we experience is not of emptiness but of the fullness of God's presence. This stillness quiets us, preparing us to know God and opening us to receive His word.

In the winter of 1980, during one of my worst wilderness periods, Laura and I took an eight-day silent retreat at the Jesuit Center for Spiritual Growth in Learning, Pennsylvania. It was a vast building built in the 1920s surrounded by gardens and fields. On this retreat, a wilderness within a wilderness, I had many encounters with God's silence as His presence. Wrapped in the embrace of His silence, He first healed Laura and me of the deep hurts we had suffered while in ministry. Then, in the silence, we heard God calling us to Taiwan as missionaries.

On the first night of the retreat I returned to my room, intent on taking to heart the director's advice about getting more rest. But I found sleep impossible. The great arched corridors, hidden chapels and dark nooks and crannies of this great house had cast their spell and beckoned me to explore. This I did until well past midnight. No one else was about. I wandered down silent hallways smelling of old wood, lighted only by flickering candles here or there, placed at the feet of the statues of Jesus and Mary. I discovered several libraries in high, vaulted rooms filled with ancient books in Latin and other languages. I crept through catacomb-like passages of earth and stone.

At last I found my way into the great chapel. My steps on the marble broke the silence with echoes from the distant arched ceiling. In the darkness I made my way toward the altar, and as I went, I ran my hands along the cool stone walls, which were interrupted every few paces by woodcarvings depicting the stations of the cross.

The altar, with its stone oblong table and golden box containing the Host, was lifted above the rest of the sanctuary by three stone steps. Above the altar was the dim outline of what I guessed to be a large crucifix. These were all the details I could make out by the smoky flame of the paschal candle. Except for my own breathing, the place was utterly silent. Outside there was no wind, only the stillness of a cold winter night.

As I surveyed my surroundings, I became conscious that beyond the darkness, amid the sacred objects—indeed, pervading the whole sanctuary, but seemingly concentrated at the altar—was the brooding presence of unfathomable mystery. I stood for a long while at the altar, feeling the mystery like a bellowing black thunderhead growing larger and larger. I had flights of wild fear, which unchecked would have caused me to flee. Yet I also experienced an ardent yearning to be penetrated wholly by the mystery, and to know its awesome depths.

Then, as if given from beyond, there came to my mind the Jesus Prayer: "Jesus Christ, Son of the living God, have mercy on me, a sinner."

I whispered the prayer in my mind, not daring to break the silence with even a prayer. I repeated it again and again, although less of it each time seemed necessary, so that after many repetitions I could speak only the name *Jesus Christ*.

His name had a great sweetness about it. It caught me up, enrapturing me. The mystery was in His name. I repeated it over and over.

Soon I began to struggle with sleep. The sense of mystery filling the place gradually released its hold on me, and I returned down the darkened corridors to my room and immediately fell fast asleep.

When we meet the silence of God, we should not speak, for there is nothing we can say worthy of disturbing it. We should instead welcome the silence, for it is like the cloud that hides God from us. His silence is the means by which His presence touches us; and when we enter into this silence, we may simply rest in it, as a child is cradled on its mother's breast.

When God is ready, He may begin to speak. It is then that we can truly listen.

Questions for Reflection

1. When has God seemed silent and you felt cut off from His presence? Can you identify any actions on your part that may have led to these times of silence?
2. If you are experiencing the silence of God now, ask the Holy Spirit to make you aware of any sin in your life. Find someone to confess your sins to. Be honest.
3. Pray through David's prayer in Psalm 51 and tailor it to your own personal sin.
4. What is the hard, long obedience to which you are called?
5. Ask God to break His silence and bless you with some word of Scripture or sign of His presence. You may also want to ask Him to confirm that you are on the right road.
6. Have you ever really met God? How?
7. Make plans to seek the silence of God's presence.

Part *two*

Battles
with Satan

Jesus, full of the Holy Spirit, returned from the Jordan, and was led by the Spirit for forty days in the wilderness, tempted by the devil.

Luke 4:1–2

We are not contending against flesh and blood, but against the principalities, against the powers, against the world rulers of this present darkness, against the spiritual hosts of wickedness in the heavenly places.

Ephesians 6:12

The Wilderness

A Place of Conflict

The wilderness is a battleground, a place where we find ourselves under attack. Assaults come from without and within. Everywhere, it seems, are enemies; everywhere, conflict and struggle.

The psalmists, men and women like ourselves, knew well the sense of being surrounded by enemies:

> Yea, dogs are round about me; a company of evildoers encircle me; they have pierced my hands and feet. . . . Save me from the mouth of the lion, my afflicted soul from the horns of the wild oxen!
>
> Psalm 22:16, 21

> Consider how many are my foes, and with what violent hatred they hate me.
>
> Psalm 25:19

51

Before entering the wilderness, I would read lines like these from the Psalms and respond, "Surely they exaggerated. Enemies everywhere? Everyone seeking to kill them? Come on, this is either paranoia or poetic license!"

In the wilderness, however, I found that it was these very psalms to which I clung for consolation. They articulated my feelings and described my own condition.

Who Are the Enemies?

In the wilderness I found enemies everywhere. These enemies came in the form of nice old ladies in the church, who with their gossip wounded me and slandered others; some of the elders, interested in position and power, who could not have cared less about the work of the Lord; and other church people, who held onto petty hurts and refused to be reconciled. My enemies even became some of those I loved most, like my own wife. They were my friends, who loved me but did not understand what I was experiencing. The enemies were Satan and his host of demons who, in the wasteland, tried to tempt and undo me. My enemy even seemed to become God Himself, who I believed was responsible for my whole situation. He was the One who had called me into the wilderness to begin with. He was the One who had sought me out, brought me into His Kingdom, blessed me with gifts and power. And now it was He who had seemingly abandoned me.

All the while, my most persistent enemy was none other than myself.

In the wilderness, although we may have conflicts aplenty with others, and others may appear to be our tormentors, in actuality they are not. They are like pawns in a much larger and more important power struggle. The contest is with Satan, with ourselves and above all with God. These are the realms of the true conflict, the place where the actual battles are won or lost.

One of the great dangers in the wilderness is to start fighting others. We can turn against our spouses, children, best friends or people in the church, while the real problem is our struggle with the devil, ourselves and God. Beware of this satanic trap of pinpointing the wrong targets.

This is not to say that the conflicts with others are not real; they are. Their resolution requires all the compassion, wisdom and courage we can muster. We may need marriage counseling or the advice of a wise pastor to help us through. We certainly need the guidance of the Holy Spirit. These conflicts will happen and need to be faced. We must recognize, however, that they are not the ultimate arenas of conflict. The rest of this book, depicting the wilderness journey, will describe the Christian's engagement in each of these three spheres of conflict.

We begin with Satan.

Introducing Satan

We may, as an article of faith, believe in Satan and evil spirits, but it is during the wilderness times that we experience their reality most vividly and suffer most from their attacks. It is also true that the more we move in the power and gifts of the Holy Spirit, the more we will experience the reality of Satan.

Scripture teaches us that Satan is created by God, yet like us is fallen. He is apparently a fallen angel. In Luke 10:18 Jesus said, "I saw Satan fall like lightning from heaven."

We often think of Satan as the radically evil enemy of God responsible for all the bad, anti-God things that happen in the world. He is—but he is more. In Scripture, as well as in our experience, we find that he is a complex being with an ambiguous nature. In some cases he acts as God's faithful servant to test and refine those whom God has called. But in other cases he is incorrigibly evil, with the sole purpose of bringing us and God's plans to ruin. In the wilderness we may meet Satan in both forms.[1]

I must confess that as I write this section, I am very uneasy. I sense that I am trespassing on the property of someone who does not like to be disturbed. At the same time, we must be very careful, when dealing with the demonic, that our imaginations do not lead us beyond the clear witness of Scripture and the use of our discursive reason. On several occasions late at night, I have started writing this section only to find that the wind howling outside got me so spooked I could not keep going. I kept seeing things in every shadow, and with each gust of wind I heard a ghost.

But the danger is real. Each time I teach on Satan or the demonic, I first pray a prayer of protection. I suggest that before you start to read these next chapters, you do the same. This is indeed a dangerous topic, in part because we invite attack, and in part because it is easy to lose balance. As C. S. Lewis observed,

> There are two equal and opposite errors into which our race can fall about the devils. One is to disbelieve in their existence. The other is to believe, and to feel an excessive and unhealthy interest in them. They themselves are equally pleased by both errors and hail a materialist or a magician with the same delight.[2]

Pray for balance and protection, then, as you proceed. Above all, recognize that Jesus has defeated Satan on the cross and that in Jesus we, too, have been given authority to defeat him.

Questions for Reflection

1. Do you believe Satan and evil spirits are real? Have you had any experiences to convince you of this reality?
2. Where are the present areas of conflict in your life? Can you identify any of them as spiritual conflict?
3. What are the different levels of meaning reflected in these conflicts? Who or what is the real enemy?
4. How has Ephesians 6:12 become real in your life?

"He was a murderer from the beginning, and has nothing to do with the truth, because there is no truth in him."
John 8:44

The Demonic

Working for Our Destruction

A murderer from the beginning! The devil and his demonic host are vile, unclean presences whose one will and intention is to overthrow all righteousness and to destroy us.

In the New Testament, a spirit of infirmity bound a woman for eighteen years (see Luke 13:10–16). A man was driven mad, cursed to a living death among the tombs by a legion of demons (see Mark 5:1–13). Demons possessing a boy caused him to fall on the ground with convulsions (see Luke 9:37–43). Satan entered Judas to cause him to betray Jesus (see John 13:27).

John Calvin summarizes what the Bible teaches us about the vicious, destructive nature of our adversary:

> We have been forewarned that an enemy relentlessly threatens us, an enemy who is the very embodiment of rash boldness, of military prowess, of crafty wiles, of untiring zeal and haste, of every conceivable weapon and of skill in the science of warfare.

55

We must, then, bend our every effort to this goal: that we should not let ourselves be overwhelmed by carelessness or faint-heartedness, but on the contrary, with courage rekindled, stand our ground in combat. Since this military service ends only at death, let us urge ourselves to perseverance.[1]

In the wilderness these descriptions of the demonic may become our own vivid reality. We may experience the devil and evil spirits as the enemy that must be fought with all the weapons at our disposal. By sowing discord, he will obstruct the work of the Church. He will muddle our discernment so we cannot see the real cause of problems. He will distort the truth and spread falsehood. In short, he will do everything possible to undo us and prevent the expression of God's Kingdom. We must rise up and, in the name of Jesus Christ, clothed with the power of the Holy Spirit, wage holy war.

As we find ourselves thrust into spiritual warfare, let us lay hold of two important truths.

First, Jesus has defeated the powers of darkness. He has given us the authority in His name to do battle with evil spirits and win. Jesus told His disciples, and I believe He tells us as well,

"Behold, I have given you authority to tread upon serpents and scorpions, and over all the power of the enemy; and nothing shall hurt you."

Luke 10:19

Jesus does not mean literal snakes and scorpions, of course. Rather, He is referring to the demonic hosts that assail us. One of the lessons to be learned in the wilderness battleground is how to use the spiritual authority we have in Christ.

The second truth to place firmly in our hearts, as we find ourselves thrust into spiritual warfare, is this: Nothing the devil does can separate us from Jesus Christ. He may lie to us and use every means possible to destroy us, but our standing in Christ cannot be swayed. It is based not on us but on God's eternal, unshakable election. Because of this truth, we have the confidence to plunge into the battle.

Putting On the Full Armor of God

No soldier is foolish enough to go into battle without being well armed. Christians likewise should be prepared when doing battle with Satan. We must put on the right kind of armor and take up weapons appropriate to our cause. Paul says, "Therefore take the whole armor of God, that you may be able to withstand in the evil day" (Ephesians 6:13).

A church I served was erupting with conflict inspired at least partly, I knew, by demons. I was terrified of this conflict, for it seemed that the church was about to blow up or collapse. Since it was my first charge right out of seminary, I had much personal insecurity bound up in this situation. I was sure my career as a minister was about to see a rapid, ignominious end.

In this state of fear and insecurity, I went to my knees in urgent prayer one night to plead with God for help. But I could not pray! All around me I felt unpleasant demonic presences. They seemed intent on distracting me, hindering my seeking the Lord. Each time I knelt and started to center my mind on Scripture, I got the peculiar sensation that there was something behind me, staring gargoyle-like over my shoulder. I glanced repeatedly behind me, only to feel that something had just left or slipped out of sight.

I was about to give up prayer and go to bed when the words from Ephesians suddenly flashed into my mind: "Take the whole armor of God." I turned to Ephesians and began slowly to read. As I did, the words began to sound more and more like a command.

Finally I said, "O.K., Lord, do You want me to put on Your whole armor? How on earth am I supposed do that?"

No answer.

Finally I said, "Then I'll just follow the instructions."

I stood up, and as I read the passage, acted it out.

"Having girded your loins with truth, and having put on the breastplate of righteousness . . ." (Ephesians 6:14).

In my imagination I vividly saw myself strapping on bright, shining pieces of armor labeled *Truth* and *Righteousness.*

"And having shod your feet with the equipment of the gospel of peace; besides all these, taking the shield of faith . . . [and] the helmet of salvation . . ." (verses 15–17).

I became aware that each piece of armor I was putting on was actually Jesus Christ, for He is our Truth, our Righteousness and our Salvation. It is in Jesus that we are safe from the devil and can defeat him.

Finally I took up "the sword of the Spirit, which is the word of God" (verse 17). It was a brilliant laser sword, Star Wars–style, and I waved it around a little. This gave me great satisfaction! I felt a little silly, as if playing a game. But as I dramatized the images that now possessed me, the exercise ceased to be just imaginary and became real. The pictures and my symbolic actions began to participate in spiritual reality.

My prayer had a remarkable effect. It calmed me, restored my strength and gave me confidence. I knew with my whole being that in the presence of the King of kings, the Light of lights, darkness has no power. And that night I was no longer bothered by presences looking over my shoulder.

The first rule in spiritual warfare, then, is to be firmly grounded in Jesus Christ, because outside of Him we are vulnerable and powerless. He alone is enough; we need nothing beyond Him. Still, I must mention the gifts and power of the Holy Spirit. They are the means by which the Lordship of Christ is expressed through us and by which we are prepared to share in building God's Kingdom.

All the supernatural gifts of the Holy Spirit are useful, but discernment and tongues have been especially useful to me. The gift of discernment is essential. Without it we are blind to the presence of the enemy, muddled as to the real source of our conflicts and confused as to the distinction between human and spiritual problems. Tongues may help us maintain prayerful openness to the guidance of the Holy Spirit. This gift also allows the power of the Spirit to flow through us.

The essential thing, however, is to be in Christ.

How do we go about doing spiritual warfare? This is not a manual to teach all the methods of spiritual warfare, but let me recount some experiences that illustrate some practical principles.

Authority in the Name of Jesus Christ

At another time in my wilderness experience, the church I served was caught up in conflict. The elders were fighting among themselves. Vicious gossip was spreading like wildfire. The congregation was close to splitting into two hostile factions. And our Sunday morning worship, symptomatic of our inward conflict, had become cold, tense and lifeless. Something oppressive seemed to have grabbed hold of the whole community and was trying to destroy it.

As pastor I did all I could to resolve the conflicts. I visited people. I pleaded with them to be reconciled. I preached sermon after sermon on God's forgiveness and love. Nothing seemed to help. The situation got more and more inaccessible to mediation—and, it seemed to me, more and more irrational.

Finally one Saturday night, I sat in my study at home dreading Sunday morning worship. I was at a loss for anything to preach.

Then the Spirit gave me a strong nudge to walk over to the sanctuary and pray.

Why not? I thought. *I've tried everything else.*

So I walked down to the church, opened the sanctuary door and started to go in. At the doorway I froze. Not only did the darkness not welcome me, but it seemed actively hostile. It was filled with oppressive, almost tangible presences. I perceived that these were the same entities that had invaded the community and our worship. I resisted a sudden rush of irrational fear that would have sent me running wildly for home.

Then, as if in counterattack, the Holy Spirit began to move me to pray in tongues. As I prayed in the Spirit, I found the courage to enter the blackness of the sanctuary. There I asked the Lord to reveal to me the names of the evil spirits that held the community in bondage. Immediately the name *hateful spirit of dissension* was thrust into my mind. Aloud I commanded the hateful thing, in the name of Jesus, to leave. The darkness swirled in resistance.

As I continued to pray, the names of many other spirits were given. In the power and authority of Jesus Christ, I commanded each one to leave. Gradually the oppressiveness in the sanctuary began to lift, replaced by the warm, sweet presence of the Holy Spirit.

I concluded my prayer time singing praises to God in tongues, and left exhilarated.

This direct confrontation with evil spirits marked a decisive turning point in our congregation. The next morning I sensed new joy and warmth about the worship. It was as if a dark cloud had lifted. Although problems persisted, we were now able to deal with them in a rational, loving manner.

We have the authority, therefore, to confront evil spirits directly and command them to leave. Ask the Holy Spirit to reveal their names to you. If it is necessary for you to know them, He will. Whether or not names are given to you, command the spirits in the name of Jesus to leave, and usually they will.[2]

To know the power of Jesus' name is a priceless lesson from the dark days in the wilderness.

Prayer and Fasting

Prayer is the most essential ingredient in spiritual warfare. Sometimes fasting is also necessary.

Once a teacher at the Bible college in Taiwan was stirring up all kinds of trouble. Clearly she had profound emotional problems, but I sensed that demons were also working through her to destroy the believers around her. I tried every way possible to minister to her and bring the situation under control, but my actions only made things worse. Personally I was coming to resent this individual.

One morning as I prayed about the situation, these words of Jesus came to mind: "This kind does not go out except by prayer and fasting" (Matthew 17:21, NIV).

The last thing I wanted to do was to give up eating on this woman's behalf! So my first response was, *O God, I don't want to waste my time fasting for that lady! You know how much I hate to fast. Is this really necessary?*

Receiving no other confirming, clear guidance, which I did not really want to receive anyway, I had a good lunch and an even better supper. But that night a strange thing happened. A friend living in Korea, whom I had told several weeks earlier about difficulties with the staff, called on the phone.

During his morning prayer time the Lord had said to him, *This kind can be cast out only by prayer and fasting.* Further, God told him to fast with me.

When my friend spoke these words, I was astonished—and a little irritated. But in the face of such obvious guidance, I overcame both my resentment of the woman and my dislike of fasting, and made a covenant with my friend to fast for three days.

As we fasted, it seemed that a dark cloud lifted and I was able to deal creatively with the woman and the staff situation. The fasting seemed to give me authority to break the evil spirit's power.

How? I must confess that as I fasted, and as the Lord forced me to confirm that I loved this woman enough to go hungry on her behalf, I was also brought to repent of things I had done to contribute to the problem.[3]

It is not that there is anything intrinsically powerful about fasting. We neither impress God nor coerce the devil by not eating. Rather, fasting is a way of focusing our attention on God and being open to Him. As we fast God may also purify us by rooting out attitudes or actions that have hindered His work through us. It is this God-centered concentration and purification that releases the power.

Spiritual Discernment through Images and Symbolic Actions

Spiritual warfare takes place in the realm of the supernatural. Normally, through the five senses, we do not have access to this realm. How, then, do we recognize the existence of evil spiritual beings? How do we know when we are in conflict with them, or what to do?

Let me say from the outset that in regard to the realities of the spirit world, without the enlightenment of the Holy Spirit, we are blind. We can act and think only as the Spirit leads us.

Each of us is different. Just as we receive the guidance of the Holy Spirit in different ways, we may also perceive the demonic in different ways. Some people receive Bible verses or words. Others go by nudges and images.

I have found pictures and symbolic actions, as given by the Holy Spirit, especially important in entering this spiritual realm. The exercise of putting on the armor of God, for instance, was both an imaginary and a symbolic action. Sometimes these image experiences can seem very strange. But if the Holy Spirit inspires them, they reflect spiritual reality.

One afternoon during the height of tension and conflict in the church I was serving, I was on my usual afternoon run. As I ran, neither prayer nor the church was in my conscious thoughts. The rhythm of the running and the familiarity of the surroundings had brought my mind to a state of neutrality.

As the road dipped down into a little valley and was just beginning to climb a steep hill, there suddenly sprang before the eye of my imagination, on the road just ahead of me, a black demonic figure. It crouched on the road with rippling muscles taut as coiled springs. Its deep-set red eyes glowed fiercely, and in its hand was a wickedly shaped spear.

With a shout I jerked one of the tall, dried weeds from the roadside and, flailing it as a weapon, went into combat.

The figure danced wildly around me, lunging toward me with its spear. I leaped about the road, wielding my own spear with all my might. As I did so, an image flashed into my mind of myself among the armies of Christ waging holy war against the supernatural forces of evil. In a moment the figure in my imagination fled. I tossed away my weapon, which was once again only a dried cane, and continued my run. I even glanced sheepishly back just to make sure none of my parishioners had seen their minister jumping around the road crazily waving a stick.

Was the picture real? I knew I had not hallucinated, yet objectively I had seen nothing but pavement and weeds. The encounter had taken place exclusively within my imagination.

The image and experience, however, revealed a profound, living inner truth. They were intensely real. It was as if an invisible spiritual reality had at that moment impinged upon my psyche and found expression in my consciousness in a vivid image. This picture was different from other daydreams in that I did not actively think it up. Rather, it thrust itself on me and came, as it were, from beyond me. I could have suppressed the image by not playing along with it. But when I let go and entered its reality, the Holy Spirit gave me a glimpse into the spiritual dynamics swirling unseen about me, in which I played a definite role.

The demonic realm as well as the angelic realm is invisible to us. When necessary, however, God may open our eyes to see into these worlds. Sometimes He does this by giving us images or symbols to make one or both of these realities visible to us. The pictures are often drawn from our cultural and educational backgrounds, as well as from Scripture. As invisible spiritual reality moves in on us, it is clothed and made visible by the images already present in our unconscious minds.

Second Kings 6:11–19 records the story of the servant of Elisha being given spiritual sight to see an image of God's powerful protection. In order to capture Elisha, the king of Syria sent horses, chariots and a large army by night to surround the city where he was staying. When the servant arose early the next morning and realized they were surrounded, he was terrified.

And the servant said, "Alas, my master! What shall we do?" He said, "Fear not, for those who are with us are more than those who are with them." Then Elisha prayed, and said, "O LORD, I pray thee, open his eyes that he may see." So the LORD opened the eyes of the young man, and he saw; and behold, the mountain was full of horses and chariots of fire round about Elisha.

2 Kings 6:15–17

The Lord indeed opened the eyes of the young man and gave him an image of divine power and might. He saw "horses and chariots of fire," which in that day symbolized military power. If God opened the eyes of the young man today, perhaps he would see a legion of angels armed with laser blasters, backed up by fleets of starships! The important thing is, when the supernatural impinges on us and we are allowed to see it through the Holy Spirit, we will view it through the lenses available to us. It is not the images themselves that are real, but the truths they embody.

In spiritual warfare, let us urgently pray Elisha's prayer for ourselves, lest we grow confused or lose hope: "O Lord, I pray Thee, open my eyes that I may see."

Cooperation with Others in Spiritual Warfare

Often the wilderness experience is characterized by a lack of fellowship, although it is in this very time that fellowship is needed most desperately. So if you lack a spiritual friend, pray for one, as a dying man crawling across desert sands prays for water. After prayer to be filled with the Holy Spirit, this is the most important petition you can make.

Without spiritual fellowship, we die of exhaustion or wander into sin and delusion. We all need someone to whom we can confess, someone who will keep us completely honest. This person is also necessary to support us in spiritual battle and assist in the discernment process.

Already you can see, from what I have shared, that in the wilderness we may encounter strange visions or feelings. We must always seek to discern their cause and meaning. They may come from the Holy Spirit, but they may also be the result of an overactive imagination, or the harbinger of a mental breakdown, or a delusion sent by Satan. Thus they must be carefully scrutinized. This is best done with the help of a trusted spiritual friend who is well grounded in Christ, knows the Scripture and is experienced in the ways of the Spirit.

A spiritual friend is also essential in the warfare itself. Jesus says:

> "Again I say to you, if two of you agree on earth about any-thing they ask, it will be done for them by my Father in heaven. For where two or three are gathered in my name, there am I in the midst of them."
>
> Matthew 18:19–20

The secret of waging successful spiritual warfare is that it must be done in the name of Jesus, and with Jesus present. This requires fellowship with other Christians.

Cooperation in spiritual combat takes many forms. The most common is two or three gathered in the name of Jesus, praying together against the power of the evil one. With others we can better discern and oppose the devil. Brothers or sisters also help to provide objective confirmation of what is going on.

Once while on a retreat, I was praying with three co-work-ers for a person with deep inner hurts. At one point we encoun-tered a demon. After I commanded it to leave, I felt a black force sweep by us suddenly as the person was liberated. To confirm that this bizarre experience was not just my imagination, I looked to one of my co-workers. She had goose bumps all over her arms. She had sensed the same thing.

Cooperating with others in spiritual warfare may take the form of two or three working together under the guidance of the Holy Spirit to cover one another's flanks. My friend who heard God's direction for us to fast is a case in point.

On another occasion, when Laura and I were living in Taiwan, I was out late one evening leading a healing meeting at a large Presbyterian church an hour and a half away in Taipei. It always seemed (and still does) that whenever I conducted some ministry under the anointing of the Holy Spirit, the devil was vicious in his attacks against my family and me, especially during wilderness times. This night was no exception.

Around eleven in the evening, as Laura waited up for me at home, she began to feel uneasy. Even though there was nothing visible, she came under attack by an evil, threatening presence.

This is a difficult experience to describe, and might only have been the result of the late hour, the empty house and her imagination. But she felt alarmed and considered calling our Canadian neighbors, Marybeth and Paul McLean, asking them to pray for her or to come over. She did not, however, because the whole thing seemed silly. After a while the presence withdrew and left the house peaceful again. Laura went to sleep. Unknown to her, God had led our neighbors to intercede for her.

A few days later we learned that at the same time Laura began to come under attack, Marybeth and Paul were praying together. Marybeth had a strong feeling that something was wrong and that they needed to pray for Laura. As they did, Marybeth received a clear vision of a dark, stooped shadow shape with a horrible hag face advancing on our house. They prayed in the name of Jesus for it to go away, and in the vision it stopped, turned around and left.

Was this imagination or reality? Like my experience on the road while running, the image received by our friends was intensely real. And by entering its reality, they played a role in combating the spiritual forces threatening Laura.

Christ-centered friends may advance with us actively in battle or they may serve as our rear guard. If you find yourself moving into a time of wilderness, with heightened spiritual warfare, ask God to raise up intercessors who will provide prayer covering for you. Then seek them out by asking Christian friends to make a covenant to uphold you in prayer. These intercessors are essential if you are to win the spiritual battles that will ambush you on the wilderness road.

Perhaps it is only a matter of perspective, but in this form of spiritual warfare the devil's actions are often directed at those around us. His goal is hindering the work of God's Kingdom. We may experience him as a malicious, destructive interference to the work of the Church. This battle may be waged outside of us and not affect us personally. But there are times in the wilderness when Satan turns his guns on us. When this happens, the focus of conflict moves from outside of us to within us. The battleground ceases to be the church or community, and now becomes our very souls.

Questions for Reflection

1. Where in your life would it be helpful to apply the principles of spiritual warfare connected to the authority of Jesus Christ in prayer and fasting?
2. Have you ever experienced a graphic image leaping spontaneously into your mind, like the demonic figure assaulting me on the road?
3. How would you confirm that such an experience participates in objective reality?
4. In prayer, seek guidance as to how you can more effectively use the authority of Jesus Christ.

7

"Simon, Simon, behold, Satan demanded to have you, that he might sift you like wheat, but I have prayed for you that your faith may not fail; and when you have turned again, strengthen your brethren."
Luke 22:31–32

Meeting the Devil as God's Tester

Is it possible that Satan can actually act as God's servant? The Bible makes it clear that he can and does.

In the first chapter of the book of Job, for example, we find Satan among the sons of God in the heavenly court. God said to him, "Have you considered my servant Job, that there is none like him on the earth, a blameless and upright man, who fears God and turns away from evil?" (verse 8). Satan responded that the reason for Job's faithfulness was that God had greatly blessed him. At this, God gave Satan permission to strip Job of all that he had, to see whether he would remain faithful.

It is clear in this story that Satan was acting not only with the permission of God, but at His suggestion. God's purpose in this case: to show Job's faithfulness.

In 1 Corinthians 5:1–5 we find another example of Satan working in God's service. In the Corinthian church a man was sleeping with his father's wife. To deal with this gross act of immorality, Paul urged the church to drive him out and "to deliver this man to Satan for the destruction of the flesh. . . ." (verse 5). He needed to be put outside the protection and support of the Body of Christ—could we say cast out into the wilderness?—so that Satan could begin his refining work in him.

Here Satan is presented as God's faithful servant who would torment this man "that his spirit may be saved in the day of the Lord Jesus" (verse 5). Apparently Satan was successful and the man repented. But in 2 Corinthians 2:5–11 we find that the church would not forgive him and welcome him back into their fellowship. Paul urged the members of the congregation to forgive and comfort him, "or he may be overwhelmed by excessive sorrow" (verse 7). If they did not forgive, Satan would gain the advantage over all of them. The situation would cease being redemptive and become merely destructive of the church and of the penitent sinner.

Peter, too, was driven into the wilderness to be tested by Satan. He was a natural leader through whom Jesus would establish His Church. But Peter did not yet know himself or the depth of sin within himself. He asserted confidently to his Master, on the night of Jesus' arrest, that "though they all fall away, I will never fall away" (Matthew 26:33). Satan knew Peter's weakness, as well as the special position of leadership to which he was called, and so demanded to have a go at this impulsive fisherman.

Satan is evil, but he was eager to perform for God the service of preparing Peter for leadership. Nor did Jesus deny Satan this privilege, for He knew that it must be. The devil accomplished in a few days what Jesus was unable to do in three years—to make Peter know himself. What a risk Jesus took, for He also knew that Peter really could fail! Most likely he would have, had Jesus not prayed for his faith not to fail.

In the denial and the time that followed, Satan worked to refine the dross out of Peter. And indeed, after Jesus restored him (see John 21:15–23), Peter was elevated as a leader among the disciples, offering comfort and guidance. After Pentecost we find the fully restored Peter speaking with power and authority for building up the Church.

Those called to spiritual leadership will arouse Satan's attention and bring him running, eager to perform his diabolical service. Jesus may let us go for a season that we may be refined and made more useful. This testing is an essential part of the wilderness experience and of growing to spiritual maturity.

We may experience Satan as tester in many different ways. I have experienced him most often as a numinous terrifying presence and as a voice.

Satan as a Numinous Evil Presence

I had a terrifying encounter with Satan one December evening while I was in college. A girlfriend and I were driving back to campus from a Christmas concert in a nearby city. I was a committed Christian, although Margie (not her real name) was not.

It was a cold, clear, moonlit evening. Rather than go straight back to our dormitories, since the night was still young, we pulled off the main road onto a dirt road that ran through an empty field. The moment we did, I felt a cold chill run through me. It took only a few moments for me to become distinctly aware of some evil presence nearby.

"Do you feel anything?" I asked.

"Yes," replied Margie in a shaky voice. "What is it?"

A force or power was instilling terror in me that made me want to run, but at the same time it was strangely drawing me. It was the sort of attraction to annihilation that one sometimes gets while looking off a high place and feeling the compelling urge to jump.

"I don't know," I replied. "But why don't we go see what it is?"

It seems incredible that I would have suggested such a foolish thing! But we both got out of the car and walked slowly down the road. Margie was clinging to me.

There was a crisp, almost brittle quality to the cold night in which details were made brilliant by a full moon. As we walked, the force got stronger. I had not yet been given the gift of tongues, so I simply prayed over and over, "Lord Jesus, protect us. Lord Jesus, protect us."

I knew we were in the presence of something radically evil. I also knew deep inside that I was safe in Christ.

Suddenly we both looked off to the right side of the road. There in the field, not more than fifty feet away, was a black shape.

Language fails me when I attempt to describe exactly what we saw. It was much bigger than a man, yet at the same time seemed concentrated in a single point. It was black on black— a blackness that sucked up and annihilated reality. It almost seemed that we were looking into a void of noncreated nothingness. The surging power emanating from this shape both repelled and attracted me.

Margie and I stopped in our tracks and, without saying a word, started to back up step by step and retreat to the car. I dared not turn and run for fear it would leap onto my back and consume me. All the while I prayed, while Margie clung desperately to me for protection.

No sooner had we taken a few steps backward than the thing began silently and slowly to glide toward us. Margie lost all control. She started screaming frantically and bolted to the car.

Something within me held firm. I retreated slowly, all the while praying and holding up my hands in command, as if to fend it off. Soundlessly the thing advanced on me, but it did not get much closer. Finally I got to the car, tore out of the place and headed back to the school as fast as I could drive.

We could see nothing now, but we could still feel the awful presence pursuing us and threatening to engulf us in its blackness. Margie screamed hysterically and struggled the whole way.

When we arrived at the campus, I drove right over the grass to the door of the college chapel. Jumping out, I dragged Margie behind me and ran to the altar, where we both fell down in front of the cross.

71

"We belong to Jesus Christ," I shouted, "and not to your darkness! In the name of Jesus Christ, be gone!"

Suddenly it was gone. Everything snapped back to normal. The little chapel. Reality. We were no longer about to be engulfed in nonexistence.

Margie and I remained in the church for a while, praying for cleansing and trying to regain our composure before returning to our dormitories.

Later, astonishingly, Margie could remember nothing of this experience. Instead she had a vague recollection that we had had some sort of fight.

This incident altered my view of reality profoundly. I think God let me confront Satan so I would know his existence experientially. There was also some refining going on. This experience of Satan may have been invited by the sinful possibilities inherent in my relationship with my girlfriend. The encounter with radical evil laid bare our souls, enabling me to see that Margie was not a suitable companion for me to share my life in spiritual ministry. The encounter also revealed my own sinful nature, which had been horribly fascinated by and actually attracted to this raw power of evil.

What is the purpose of such a terrifying experience? Usually in this life, good and evil are muddled. We see neither in their pure forms. But I believe God gave me a glimpse into the abyss that lies at the end of all roads of disobedience to God's gracious, life-giving will and intention. God let me see the radical nature of evil, in contrast to the vitality and life of His presence. To catch such a glimpse destroys complacency about the security of existence! Life is not secure at all, but threatened with evil. And after one look at evil in its distilled form, the message is clear: Choose life. Choose Jesus Christ.

I have met this same presence on several other occasions, each vivid and terrifying. On each occasion, others along with me perceived the presence as objectively "out there." And during each instance, unlike my experience in college, I felt no panic, only a firm resting in Jesus Christ and moving against

Satan in the authority given by Christ. The evil presence, under these circumstances, was unable to congeal into the concentrated being, the engulfing shape, that it had with Margie and me that December night. Each incident, moreover, has served to refine me and the others who experienced it.

One evening, for example, as I was about to commence the process of becoming an ordained minister, I was to meet with the presbytery and come under their care. Laura and I, engaged to be married, were sitting in a parked car outside the church, praying and waiting for the meeting to begin.

Suddenly, just as in the field, I felt the same life-annihilating evil presence near the car. I turned to Laura and said, "Do you feel anything?"

"Yes!" she shouted joyfully. "Praise God! Hallelujah! We belong to Jesus Christ, who is the victor!"

Instantly the evil presence departed.

That night the Lord sealed in my heart a certainty that Laura was the helpmate who was to walk with me into the spiritual adventures ahead. I also knew once again that Satan was real and that he was viciously opposed to my going into the ministry.

Thank God such encounters like these are not common! But if you have one, hold fast to Jesus Christ and take authority over the malevolent entity in His name. Command it to be gone. Afterward search your soul and reflect why this could have happened. Ask the Holy Spirit to reveal to you what you are to learn from such a terrible experience—about yourself, about reality and about God.

Usually, however, we experience the devil in a far more subtle way—as a voice speaking through our own thoughts that tempts and condemns us.

Satan as a Voice

Throughout the Bible Satan talks to men and women.

> Now the serpent was more crafty than any of the wild animals the LORD God had made. He said to the woman. . . .
>
> Genesis 3:1, NIV

73

The tempter came to him and said. . . .

Matthew 4:3, NIV

If we have done something wrong or have fallen short of our own expectations, Satan accuses us relentlessly. "See, you're no good," he says. "You'll never do it. God can never use a person like you. You aren't good enough to serve Him, you fool!" Or, "Look at your sin. Look at all you've done. You can never be forgiven. You might as well give up on being good and just enjoy the sin." Usually what the devil says has a good bit of truth about it and would be completely true if our righteousness were based on ourselves and not on Christ.

Or Satan may speak to us denying the reality of what God is doing. When I first prayed to receive the infilling with the Holy Spirit, I had a great experience of anointing and started spontaneously to speak in tongues. As it was happening, I knew without a doubt that it was real. But the moment I left the place of prayer, a nagging voice started whispering in my mind, *You fool, you were deceived. That wasn't real; it was fake. Those nonsense noises—they weren't really tongues. God didn't really bless you like that; that was an illusion.* Soon the wonderful assurance that I had just received was overcome by a thousand doubts.

Or Satan may whisper to us, encouraging us to step into some sin. Rarely does he invite us to some gross sin—at least at first. Usually he extends temptation by degrees, until he traps us into doing what we never thought possible: "Come on, one drink won't hurt you," or, "Just this once, twisting the truth is actually for everyone's benefit." The old snake knows that if he were to suggest some obvious evil, we would resist him stoutly. So he uses little, "inconsequential" things to start us on the path to hell.

During a Dunamis conference, I kept noticing one of the members of the prayer team. I had known and appreciated her for years, but was particularly conscious one morning of how pretty she was. So I thanked God that I had such a beautiful sister, and went on with teaching and ministry. Usually that tactic works for me as a protection against temptation.

Then I became aware of the voice, subtly connecting with my own fallenness. *Wouldn't it be wonderful to sleep with her?* "Oh, shut up!" I said. "Get lost, in the name of Jesus Christ!" But the thoughts persisted all day.

Later I felt the Holy Spirit nudging me to drag these thoughts out into the light by confessing them to Tom Naylor, who was sharing the teaching with me. But I was embarrassed to do so. The issue seemed inconsequential. Besides, I was not going to do anything inappropriate, so why bother with the embarrassment of confession?

It was here, by seeing this temptation as inconsequential and not talking to Tom, that I fell into Satan's strategy to defeat me. If I had confessed to Tom, the battle would have been over, for Satan would have been exposed. But under the cover of secrecy, the subtle battle persisted.

St. Ignatius affirmed that the devil gets the upper hand by working in the dark. From the rules for discerning spirits, here is Rule 13:

> Our enemy may also be compared in his manner of action to a false lover. He seeks to remain hidden and does not want to be discovered. If such a lover speaks with evil intention to the daughter of a good father, or to the wife of a good husband, and seeks to seduce them, he wants his words and solicitations kept secret. He is greatly displeased if his evil suggestions and depraved intentions are revealed by the daughter to her father, or by the wife to her husband. Then he readily sees he will not succeed in what he has begun. In the same way, when the enemy of our human nature tempts a just soul with his wiles and seductions, he earnestly desires that they be received secretly and kept secret. But if one manifests them to a confessor, or to some other spiritual person who understands his deceits and malicious designs, the evil one is very much vexed. For he knows that he cannot succeed in his evil undertaking, once his evident deceits have been revealed.[1]

Satan knows I am happily married, in love with Laura and that I have built a moral fortress with lines I absolutely will not cross. So the old snake changed his tactics.

Just tell her she is absolutely beautiful in that dress, he whispered.

She really was lovely in that dress! Normally, as a brother in Christ, I would have given the compliment. Whenever my wife, one of my daughters or a co-worker is wearing something attractive, I am in the habit of telling them. Life is too short not to tell people how much you love and appreciate them. But on this occasion, something was different in me, and I knew that to give the compliment would not spring from the right motivation on my part. So I stoutly resisted.

At the end of the meeting, as everyone was leaving, I ignored the voice that was nearly shouting in my head. *Just tell her now; you'll miss the opportunity to bless her!* Instead I gave her a big hug and thanked her for sharing with Tom and me in ministry.

But Satan must have been working on her as well. After everyone else had left, she came running back to tell me about a word from the Lord she had received for me. This time, as she turned to go, I said, "You know, you really are beautiful in that dress!"

She looked flattered, thanked me for the compliment and left.

Immediately my conscience smote me. I knew I had stepped over a subtle but clear boundary line. I was light years away from actually committing adultery, but Satan's voice, in collaboration with my own flesh, had tempted me successfully to take a small step in that direction. An action that would normally have been innocent had in this case crossed the line, and I knew it in the pit of my soul.

Immediately I went and confessed my sin to Tom, who prayed for me and brought words of forgiveness. The struggle ceased, and the next day, while in deliverance ministry, I simply appreciated this prayer warrior as a lovely sister in the Lord.

I also kicked myself for the whole stupid battle! It could have been prevented if I had brought it into the light, when I first started hearing the voice, by asking Tom to pray for me. Instead I played with fire by succumbing to an "inconsequential" temptation.

Resisting the Voice

In the wilderness it often seems that God's Word is silent and our perception of His will muddled, while the voice of Satan is relentless and crystal clear. Our life in Christ grows tasteless and dull, while our tendency to sin becomes an almost irresistibly sweet compulsion.

James 4:7 says, "Resist the devil and he will flee from you." He does flee when we resist him with a whole heart. But when we give him an ear or yield to his suggestions, he starts to control us and becomes harder to resist.

In the wilderness, especially during times of meaninglessness, I have had to fight a constant battle against Satan's voice.

During one period, when the work of ministry had become meaningless and boring for me, it seemed that I did the same stupid things day after day. I sensed no direction and found nothing to rouse my interest. I did not want to pray. I read the Bible not for my own nourishment but only because I had to come up with something to preach on Sunday.

In this state of emptiness, I began to struggle with lust. Unrestrained sexual fantasies seemed a natural way to fill up the vacuum of my life. I found myself sexually attracted to several of the women in the church.

One gray winter day I set out for my daily run on the back-country roads behind our house. As I ran, I glanced down over an embankment and caught sight of a magazine page emblazoned with a nude female figure. I stopped in my tracks. At once there arose within me a great storm of debate.

One side argued, *No, don't stop. Leave it there and keep on running.*

The other side, tingling with excitement, rebutted, *Oh, don't be a fool! Go ahead, what'll it hurt? There's no harm in just looking at some pictures.*

The good side retorted, *Come on now, in your state of mind, that's the last thing you need. Just run on!*

But then my tempter said, *Look, you're a minister of the Gospel. You really need to have a look and see how wicked this stuff really is. Here's your chance to see firsthand the depths to which American society has fallen.*

The old snake! That was the argument that won the day. I told myself, *I'll have a quick look, then destroy it, lest some child find it.*

So I climbed down the bank and picked the magazine up. It was a *Hustler* nearly buried in the dead leaves. Lest anyone see me, I slipped it under my shirt. The possibility of being seen, except by a few lonely cows, was remote and I knew it. But a guilty conscience feels eyes everywhere.

I trotted on, found a hidden place off the road, sat down and consumed the pictures greedily. They were far more explicit and erotic than I had expected. No sooner had I glanced at the first few pages than I was captivated. Lust knew no bounds.

Finally I hid my treasure carefully under some leaves, smothered my nagging guilt with pleasure and ran home.

That should have been the end of the episode, but it was not. For the next several days that magazine exercised an incredible power over me. It dominated my thoughts and aroused my passions. All I could think about was sex. I saw every woman not as a person but as a sex object. I had one single-minded obsession: to return and feast my eyes on those pictures. I had no desire for communion with God, nor could I prepare my sermon for Sunday.

I should end the story here, but I fear that my reader will be left with the impression that Satan bound me completely. By God's grace, he did not. Within a few days the Holy Spirit entered my prison and called me to regain my freedom.

For freedom Christ has set you free, He whispered. *But is this freedom? Is being possessed, and being so driven by these base thoughts that you cannot contemplate the holy, freedom? You*

must return and destroy that magazine. Otherwise it will con-
tinue to feed your lust.

I resisted obeying. It had been pleasant to escape being holy
and to get out from under God's law. But I knew in the depths
of my soul that sin, even though pleasant at first, would pro-
duce bitter fruit if left to grow.

Finally, on an afternoon run a few days later, I returned to
the hiding place, swept away the dead leaves and brought out
the magazine. It is not to my credit that I took one last look at
the pictures. But to my surprise I found that they had completely lost their power to attract me. In fact, they disgusted me,
and I felt sorry for the women who had to make money this
way. My obedience was already beginning to yield the sweet
fruits of freedom.

I drowned the magazine in the rapids of a rushing stream,
and as I did I experienced the cleansing, liberating work of the
Holy Spirit.

What Are Your Areas of Weakness?

This experience dealt with the sin of lust, but it could as well
have been about anger, revenge or doubt. Just add your particular sin to make it applicable to your own situation. Each of
us has built within the structure of our own personality a tendency to sin in a particular manner. This is the point where the
walls of our defenses are the weakest.

St. Ignatius' Rule 14 for discerning spirits confirms the persistent tactic of Satan to discern our weakness and launch his
attacks there:

> The conduct of our enemy may also be compared to the tac-
> tics of a leader intent upon seizing and plundering a position he
> desires. A commander and leader of an army will encamp,
> explore the fortifications and defenses of the stronghold, and
> attack at the weakest point. In the same way, the enemy of our
> human nature investigates from every side all our virtues, the-
> ological, cardinal, and moral. Where he finds the defenses of

eternal salvation weakest and most deficient, there he attacks and tries to take us by storm.[2]

The devil's attacks on our areas of weakness may take many clever turns, as his beguiling voice seeks to make us stumble. The lust attack was a direct assault on my own weakness. If someone else has a sensuous nature, Satan may push that person beyond simple love and compassion until he or she, too, is consumed by lust. With others Satan's method is to detect the direction of their good tendencies and then push them to the extreme until they fall. Another person is neat and orderly and seeks to do everything possible to fulfill the Law of God. Such a person may be pushed to become a narrow-minded perfectionist or legalist.

In all these attacks, the devil is playing his role as God's tester or sifter. He does this by laying before us options other than obedience to God's Word. After suggesting alternative possibilities to us, he compels us to choose. In such a way he forces us to grow and become free and responsible people. We must decide for Satan or for God. Through the good offices of Satan, we may also begin to see ourselves as we really are. He accuses us of our sin and guilt and tells us clearly that in our own righteousness, we have no standing with God.

If we consistently reject the devil's leading and choose for God, Satan does indeed flee. He has no power over us and we emerge from the struggle with a deeper faith, a refined character and a stronger resolve to follow Christ. In such a way Satan has served God and us well. If, on the other hand, we give in to his temptations, we sell ourselves into his power. Then he torments us no end. Here, too, the devil serves as God's instrument—but now for our destruction.

In the wilderness you will, like Jesus and a host of others, meet Satan. In the battles that will rage, hold onto Jesus Christ with all your strength, lest you fall into the abyss. The purpose of God's terrible wilderness is to allow you to be tested until your own strength fails and any delusions of your own goodness are shattered. Then, as you are falling, you will discover that Jesus is there holding you with an eternal grip and imparting to you His own blood-bought authority to defeat Satan.

Questions for Reflection

1. How have you experienced Satan?
2. How have you been tempted by Satan? What particular areas are you presently dealing with?
3. What are your weak points?

Part *three*

Struggles
with
Ourselves

Wilderness as the Place to Know Ourselves

Search me, O God,
and know my heart;
test me and know my
anxious thoughts.
Psalm 139:23, NIV

When we meet Satan as our sifter, we also begin to meet ourselves. Because the fact is, the devil never makes us do anything. He only urges us to actualize the evil potential already present within each of us. The testing work of Satan compels us to know ourselves and our need for utter dependence on Jesus Christ.

Such knowledge, however, does not come easily. It must penetrate many defenses. Culture, education, family, achievements—all are forged by our egos into armor to protect the fragile, vulnerable persons we are inside. In society we wear masks that hide our real fears and desires. We become the roles that have been imposed on us: mother, doctor, student, pastor, troublemaker, spouse, saint, whatever. We conform to the images and the images become us. Each of us has a carefully constructed self-concept that is partly true, in that it is based

85

on real potential within us, but at the same time false, because it is usually too good (or perhaps too bad) and thus prevents us from seeing our true selves.

Who are you really? Do you know yourself? Imagine for a moment that you suddenly found yourself transported to another world. You are met by the creatures of that world, who ask you, "What are you?" Tell them your name. What does that mean? Tell them where you are from. No use!

When we really start to ponder that question, don't we face a mystery camouflaged by many illusions? With others it is the same. They may grow familiar and predictable, but can we ever really know them?

Years ago I was acquainted with a saintly old couple who opened their home to students. After the man's wife of fifty years passed away, he told the other students and me with tears in his eyes, "I lived with her, slept with her and had six children by her. We prayed together, laughed together and cried together. But who was this person who graced my life these fifty years? I knew her deeply, but I never grasped the mystery of who she really was. Now she's gone."

This is true of others and of us as well.

In our relationship with God, we are even more hopelessly trapped in illusion and confronted with mystery. What is the nature of our faith? Is it really faith or is it a habit of thought inherited from our parents? Of what does our relationship with our Creator consist? Is it a living relationship with a God who is real or is it just a set of ritual observances, learned dogma and moral scruples that neatly define the world and provide us with security? Have we met God in His reality or have we met only the literary or cultural expression of His reality? Who is He really—this Being who spun out galaxies, reveals Himself as Trinity and died on the cross?

What of our own righteousness? Have we met that radical evil within ourselves for which Christ had to die? Or do we pretend we are somehow worthy of God's love? Do we not fear that if we were really known, we would be found unworthy of love even by ourselves?

Most of us protect ourselves from true knowledge of self and genuine encounters with the living God. It is well that we do, for such knowledge is terrible. But to gain such knowledge is the secret of spiritual growth and the path to usefulness in the Kingdom of God. Being brought to a knowledge of ourselves that shatters illusions is the first step to knowing God. And knowing God is the only way to truly know ourselves.

John Calvin described the interconnectedness of these two kinds of knowledge:

> Nearly all the wisdom we possess, that is to say, true and sound wisdom, consists of two parts: the knowledge of God and of ourselves. But while joined by many bonds, which one precedes and brings forth, the other is not easy to discern. In the first place, no one can look upon himself without immediately turning his thoughts to the contemplation of God, in whom he "lives and moves" (Acts 17:28). . . . Again, it is certain that man never achieves a clear knowledge of himself unless he has first looked upon God's face, and then descends from contemplating him to scrutinize himself.[1]

To teach us both knowledge of Himself and knowledge of ourselves, God may drive us into the brutal school of the wilderness.

For each Christian the time in the wilderness will be different. But for most it is a period in which we meet the silence of God and deal with great loneliness, frustration, confusion, temptation or failure. The purpose of these struggles: to peel away the outer, protective layers of security that have provided meaning, purpose and identity in our lives, but which also protect us from true knowledge of self and of God. As this protection is stripped away, we begin to experience our souls' nakedness and know the forces of good and evil swirling in the depths of our beings.

It is then, while standing ultimately vulnerable, that God may consume us with His fiery love. We see with clarity of vision His majesty and power. We begin to know the mystery of His reality and presence in a way no words or doctrine can contain. We hear Him calling us to a special work in the Kingdom that will transform both us and the world.

I must affirm again and again, however, that this aspect of the wilderness is fraught with danger. One may come undone. Without the firm anchors of the Word of God and the Church, it is easy to drift from orthodoxy. We may be battered to and fro by the power of our own experiences. In the inner depths of ourselves are strange creatures whose seductive beauty or terrifying appearance may lead us away from the God who loves us.

This and the next phases of wilderness are even more perilous than the battles with Satan. Here the enemy becomes first ourselves and then God. So if you know you are entering such a period, chain yourself, like a man cast overboard on a wild, storm-blown sea, to the Scriptures as a life raft and seek protection in the Body of Christ.

In what follows, I will describe some of the false ideas that must be struck down before we can begin to see God, our ministry and ourselves clearly.

Questions for Reflection

1. Who are you really?
2. Do you have a sense of why are you here and what the purpose of your existence is?
3. Are you willing to take the risk of asking God to reveal to you who you are in His light?
4. Take the risk. Pray, "God, show me who I am."

9

> "Truly, truly, I say to you, unless a grain of wheat falls into the earth and dies, it remains by itself alone; but if it dies, it bears much fruit."
> John 12:24, NASB

Dying to Illusions

God sends us into the wilderness for one terrible purpose: to kill us. The first thing He puts to death is our false ideals about ourselves, Him and our relationship with Him. He kills those things that give us a false spirituality so we can grow into an authentic relationship with Him.

When Jesus met the woman at Jacob's well, He had to kill her illusions and false ideals. When she said, "I have no husband," the Lord exposed the whole truth: "You are right when you say you have no husband. The fact is, you have had five husbands, and the man you now have is not your husband. What you have just said is quite true" (John 4:17–18, NIV).

Then Jesus dealt with her false Samaritan spirituality that fixed the worship of God on their holy mountain:

> "Believe me, woman, a time is coming when you will worship the Father neither on this mountain nor in Jerusalem. . . .

89

Yet a time is coming and has now come when the true worshipers
will worship the Father in spirit and truth, for they are the kind
of worshipers the Father seeks. God is spirit, and his worshipers
must worship in spirit and in truth."

verses 21, 23–24, NIV

Having had these false ideas about herself and God struck
down, she was ready to meet Jesus as who He really was.

In the same way, Jesus Christ in the wilderness will destroy
our illusions so we may truly know ourselves and Him. These
are not simply adjustments in our thinking; they amount to a
personal encounter with the Lord of the universe. Meeting Him
destroys our illusions and blows away what is false.

Dying to Overdependence on Others

The gift of community comes from God. When we are born
into His Kingdom, we are born into a family with other brothers and sisters. We are connected to a body—the Body of Christ,
the Church. As we grow in faith, we depend on those who have
gone before and those who now walk with us. We have all
depended on a close friend or wise pastor to help us grow. And
we need corporate worship, prayer and study to shape and sustain our faith. Accountability to others helps us be obedient to
God and remain faithful to a life of prayer and Bible study.

But we may begin to depend on others too much, so that our
relationship with God and our experience of Him is not really
our own, but a socially conditioned reality based on the support and expectations of others.

When I lived in Korea, the Reverend Archer Torrey of Jesus
Abbey was a spiritual father to me. Through him I experienced
God. And at seminary I enjoyed wonderful fellowship. The
structure of seminary and church life provided social support
for my faith. But in the wilderness all this was pulled away. I
had no community, no one to turn to. People were looking to
me to support their faith. But to whom was I to look?

With community gone, I found that I had to stand alone, and I could not. My faith began to wither. My prayer times lost their sweetness and became lifeless routine. It was as if the Lord not only removed me from fellowship with other Christians, but He stepped away, too. A time of spiritual famine showed me just how dependent on others I had become.

The challenge of the wilderness is to stand alone and to walk with God. In this way faith becomes our own, not something secondhand. Afterward, when God returns us to the life of fellowship, we can better contribute to its sustenance.

Dying to Isolation and Pride

Spiritual leadership is a lonely calling. Those who have been especially touched by the Holy Spirit, who have passed through great suffering or who have been possessed by a fierce love for God and find themselves driven by a heavenly vision, often find themselves alone. Their experience has sent them into new realms of reality. Their imaginations have been ignited by vision and yearnings that lose their fire when articulated in common language.

To have been given a vision of the Kingdom of God is to have been cursed to a life of restless striving to make this earth and oneself conform to the vision. Part of the pain is lacking the gifts or opportunity to fully live the new reality. Thus, the vision remains partly enclosed in the bondage of one's limitations.

All this makes for vast loneliness. Spiritual adventure, although it deepens us, widens the gap between us and the common culture, with its trite, media-dominated modes of communication and its safe, packaged experiences.

Once I was especially tormented with loneliness. Not only did I have no one with whom I could share my heart, but the vision of God's work burning in me seemed like an utter impossibility. It was a burden, a curse. Life and ministry would have been much easier directed by common sense rather than by this impossible call from God.

Following is a poem I wrote about being torn between two worlds—a dialogue between me and the source of spiritual vision:

O Thou cursed Vision
that opened my eyes to realms beyond
and blinded me by Thy brilliant light!

Now, having seen the sun, can I dwell within the land of
  shadows
and join the common charade of proclaiming them real?

O Thou cursed Vision,
Thou hast given me new tongues
and tuned my ears to apprehend new songs.
What blessing, to join the mystic choruses of sun, moon and
  stars and the hosts of heaven!
What exalted melodies, what exquisite harmonies, what
  penetrating rhythms!

What delight!
Except I am cast out of the common babble.
My notes all seem out of key, as if struck from strangely
  different chords—
yet whose is the tongue that is out of key?

Take heart, my child.
Hold fast to thy new sight.
Slip not again into blindness, nor crawl forever back amid the
  shadows.
Bend not thy knee with the idolatrous crowd
that exalts them as real, as true, as light.
For thine eyes have been touched as the prophets' eyes were
  touched.
You must live as they lived,
cast adrift between two worlds,

wandering down lonely paths
with hands reaching upward to touch the stars, yet feet still
  earthbound,
restlessly compelled to speak words that few will understand.
Yes, my child, share their loneliness,
share their curse,
yet share their blessing.

This poem, "O Thou Cursed Vision," is a little overintense, I suppose, but in the wilderness it was the cry of my soul. This sort of talk is dangerous and carries with it the temptation to spiritual pride. That is the charge often leveled against those of all ages who have been touched by the Holy Spirit: that they have become spiritual elitists. They are claiming (so it is said) some special experience or access to God out of reach to the ordinary person.

This charge is often true, but it does not have to be. One of the challenges of the wilderness is to live in the loneliness, to let the isolation strip away our socially conditioned faith, that authentic faith may blossom. But the challenge is also to resist the natural tendencies to isolation and pride.

Through deep, Christ-centered love, reaching out to others in community, we can learn to be open to the diverse ways the Spirit works in different people. Religious experience gives us no special claim to God, but instead lays on us greater responsibility. We must learn how to share the vision and experience, for if authentic, they do not separate but unite, touching the same God-inspired but inarticulate yearnings or restlessness in others. The vision of the Kingdom of God, if true, will stir others, for the reality of the Kingdom is not some special possession of the spiritual elite, but the heritage of all God's children.

The task of those who have passed through the wilderness is to learn how to speak in language that can be understood. Let's be guided by the love of Christ, which calls us beyond ourselves to others. Following Christ will lead us up the mountain in prayer where we may have mystical experiences, then back down into the valley, where we follow the same Christ in communicating the reality we have seen.

Dying to Techniques and Attitudes

Often those who have been empowered by the Holy Spirit have a strong sense of God's presence. In the Holy Spirit as Emmanuel, "God with us," the Almighty is indeed near. But with this joyful revelation comes the subtle temptation to think God has become controllable or manageable.

I have often laid hands on people in prayer and seen them tremendously blessed. They may pray in tongues or receive deep inner healing or even see a vision of Christ. When this happens I am astonished that God can use me. But I am sometimes tempted to think that by laying hands on a person and praying in the "right" way, I can actually control God.

Anyone who has experienced the power of the Holy Spirit faces the same temptation. We may be nudged to believe that through praying in tongues, fasting or quoting the right Scripture, we can get God to act according to our expectations.

This is false.

I am going to press this a little further, for not only those moving in the gifts of the Holy Spirit confront this temptation. There is great interest at present in spiritual disciplines and spirituality. We are urged to practice exercises like Bible study, prayer, worship, tithing and fasting, which prepare us for true communion with God. To be sure, these are good habits to develop. But they, too, may become false spirituality. We may be inclined to think that experiencing God's presence and blessing through the spiritual disciplines is a trick we can learn that will bring God close to us. If we meditate on the right image, keep up a daily quiet time, claim the appropriate promises from Scripture or use the right kind of prayer, we will automatically be tuned in to God.

This, too, is false.

Often God does honor our laying on of hands or participating in spiritual disciplines. He does indeed answer our prayers and speak through His Word. But in no way do we control Him, and there is nothing in us that compels Him to draw near to us. In the wilderness God strips away our false piety and expectations and shows us our naked dependence on Him, even for the very desire to be spiritual.

While on a Jesuit retreat some years ago, I started learning for the first time about spiritual consolations—movements of the Holy Spirit within us that bring joy, revelation or, best of all, a sense of God's presence.[1] When a consolation begins, it is usually so subtle that we hardly notice it. But if we become sensitive to it and are willing to let it continue, not quenching it by seizing on it with an analytical mind, it will grow in intensity.

My first consolation came one morning while I was reading my spiritual journal full of accounts of God's grace toward me. Suddenly I became aware of joy welling up inside me. I relaxed and let it wash over me like a wave. Before long I was so filled with rapture that I found myself singing a hymn at the top of my voice, "What Wondrous Love Is This!" Finally the joy transcended English and I continued in tongues. What began as a small spring had become a rushing river.

The morning's experience led me to believe I was getting the knack of being spiritual. At last, I thought, I was learning how to go with the flow of the Spirit and let the consolations come. It was exciting! I had learned a new technique for giving myself spiritual experiences.

God put an end to that fancy. After a break from the work of prayer, I had lunch and a short nap. Then I settled in my room for another hour of prayer. Placing the cross clearly in view, I waited expectantly for the Lord's presence. Spiritually I felt nothing. The only thing that happened was my back began to hurt. I prayed for a while but heard nothing. So I started reading the words from my journal that in the morning had so moved me. Now they sounded as if they were written by someone else, with no special meaning for me at all.

After what seemed like an hour, I glanced at my watch, to discover that only three or four minutes had passed.

I worked more at praying. I got on my knees, read Scripture, reread my journal, even sang "What Wondrous Love is This" again, all to no avail. Then, after thirty minutes of this tedium, I decided to call it quits and go for a run, disgusted with myself for not being able to experience God's presence.

On the way outside, I stopped at the men's room. As I sat there transacting some mundane business, I became aware of the full, awesome silence of the Lord's presence.

In a silly way I was embarrassed that He should see me in such an impious position. Then again, it was He who created me with such a necessity. Out of the silence He spoke, His words penetrating my consciousness and leaving a deep impression. (Because they were personal, I will not record them here.) Then I finished in the bathroom and went on my run, overjoyed at the words spoken but humbled at the realization that, through spirituality, I had actually attempted to control God.

It is not only through techniques that we may attempt to manage God, but through our attitudes. Sometimes we assume that our spirituality is our own possession, giving us special access to God. This is false. Even our spirituality does not come from us. It, too, is a gift from God.

During one of my wilderness times, God seemed to withdraw His presence and power. Although I laid hands on people and prayed for them, nothing happened. My prayers seemed nothing more than talking to myself. Finally even the desire to pray started to die within me.

One morning I came to my prayer time so dry that I did not care that I was dry. I was coming out of sheer force of habit, with no sweetness or hope of receiving anything. But as I knelt and opened the Scriptures, I was filled, suddenly and spontaneously, with a burning, consuming desire to know God. My heart ached to know Him as He really is. I found myself praying urgently, *God, who are You? Who are You really? Please let me know You!*

As I waited in expectant silence, I perceived within myself a depth of stillness and peace. Like wind blowing from the mouth of a cave, so out of this depth there blew an essence that included, yet transcended, me. In this depth I knew I was in the presence of the deepest mystery in the whole universe. God was showing me Himself—yet not Himself at all, but only the tremor of His passing, just as He had shown Moses, hiding in the cleft of the rock, only His back as He passed by.

This momentary consolation made a lasting impression. My heavenly Father, in this unexpected revelation, not only gave me a taste of Himself as unknowable, utterly transcendent mystery, but He taught me that even the desire for Him was not something I had the power to muster within myself. In subtle ways I had continued to believe that in managing my own spirituality, I could manage God. Now I knew that He was the Lord, never to be mastered, manipulated or controlled.

In the wilderness, when all our spirituality proves empty and when we no longer experience power, we may learn that God is the Lord. True spirituality and empowered ministry begin only when all our illusions of controlling God die and we are left helpless before Him, acknowledging that even our desire to love Him is not our own.

Questions for Reflection

1. Ask God to shatter your illusions about yourself and Him.
2. In what areas are you lying to yourself?
3. Where in your thoughts or actions have you tried to control or manipulate God?
4. Ask God to show you your utter helplessness in reaching out to Him.

10

And if I have
prophetic powers,
and understand all
mysteries and all
knowledge, and if I
have all faith, so as to
remove mountains,
but have not love,
I am nothing.
1 Corinthians 13:2

Learning
the Ministry
of Love

What is our real ministry as believers?

If you have been filled with the Holy Spirit for power and gifts, you may be tempted to think that it is evidence of the Holy Spirit's power—power to enable people to experience emotional and physical healing, authority to cast out demons, boldness to witness effectively for Jesus. Others define ministry in terms of the struggle for justice. One's political stance is what is important. One must be involved in protest or in raising the consciousness of the oppressed about their oppression. Still others see ministry as being a "successful" pastor or church administrator. They strive to have a fine choir, a packed sanctuary, an active women's group and a thriving youth program. They seek the status of serving on the most powerful committees of their churches.

All these activities are important, but are they the most important? Are any of them really the heart of ministry and the way we can be effective servants of God's Kingdom?

I had always focused on power and results. I wanted to see the Kingdom of God—with its justice, wholeness and peace—fill the earth. I longed to see the glory of God cover the earth as the waters cover the sea. After experiencing the infilling work of the Holy Spirit, I knew God could change lives and work miracles. When the Holy Spirit moved, I knew it could be dramatic and exciting. We can see clear evidence that God is present and mighty. He is a miracle-working God. (Let all the people raise their hands and shout, "Amen!") He is a God who can answer your prayers. (Hallelujah!) He is a God for whom nothing is impossible. (Amen!) I knew the Gospel could go forth in signs and wonders, as recorded in Acts, because I had seen a move of the Holy Spirit on the mission field in which there were incredible signs and wonders.

Oh! But then I arrived in the wilderness—my time in the parish. I met the Jesus who still works miracles but who did not come down from the cross. I bumped up against the reality that certain problems on this earth do not get solved. At times there is evidence of neither the power nor the presence of God. I found myself in the desert, where God seemed to have forgotten Pentecost.

My parishioners were country people. Their God was not the God of power and might, moving dramatically for global mission. He was the God of small things: the birth of a baby, the changing seasons, growing old. He was the God of those who did not throw away their crutches, but day after day found the strength to walk with them.

When I met this God in the wilderness, my theology crashed against the rock of reality and I discovered that my focus on power and miracles was incomplete. God is indeed the God of miracles, but deeper still He is the God of suffering love. The real nature of ministry, I learned, is obeying and serving, not just with Pentecostal power but with the love of Christ.

The Lord taught me this the hard way—after all my programs failed. The elders had approved my new evangelism program but nothing happened. My parish visitation program crumbled in one night. My attempts to make worship livelier through contemporary music were all vetoed. My new Sunday school program was tried for one or two Sundays, then rejected in favor of the old material. After I preached on my favorite topic, the power of the Holy Spirit, everyone said, "Nice sermon, preacher," but no one was interested. Except for the gifts of tongues as a personal prayer language, it seemed that the Lord had stopped working through me in the dramatic ways I had come to expect.

After such persistent failure, I was discouraged and ready to quit. I had blown it as a pastor, and apparently as a "Spirit-filled" Christian as well.

It was at this low point that God intervened and taught me the basics of doing His ministry.

The Secret of Ministry

There was a woman in my church whose beautiful, 23-year-old daughter had a kidney disease that, day by day, was reducing her to an emaciated invalid. Many specialists were called but their prognoses were always the same: She had only a short time to live. Many ministers had prayed for her; one had even anointed her with oil and prayed over her in tongues. But she continued to die.

I, too, laid hands on her and prayed fervently for a miracle. I really expected God to do something dramatic! But there was no miracle, and my unanswered prayers only deepened the sense of despair that filled the family.

This intractable situation was exacting a terrible toll on the girl's loving parents. They were being crushed. Week after week the mother came to our Wednesday prayer meeting and raised the same requests: for her daughter, healing; and for herself, grace to get through the week.

The situation was taking a toll on me as well. I was growing increasingly uncomfortable because this mother did not conform to my program of demonstrating that God does heal through the Holy Spirit. To me she reflected my glaring failure as a Holy Spirit–empowered minister, as well as the failure of my theology.

After one prayer meeting, while standing in the church parking lot, I forced myself to go over and ask how she was doing. I knew exactly how she was doing and, to tell the truth, dreaded hearing about the same old stuff. In response to my concern, the woman began to rehearse the same tragic story she had recounted to everyone in the church hundreds of times before.

There are some circumstances we must endure, and their immensity so captivates us that only as we tell them again and again do we regain the transcendence to master them. Still, I started feeling fidgety.

As the mother spoke, her eyes grew misty with tears. Then she began to weep.

I put my arm around her and prayed in my heart for something meaningful to say. All my proposed pastoral responses sounded hollow. So I just stood there awkwardly, silenced by her sobs.

As I did, a mysterious thing began to happen. Some power or force seemed to be playing elusively around us. A dark brooding began to come over me. Then I had the almost tangible sensation of an enormous load being lifted from her shoulders onto my own. It was a terrible, crushing weight. My heart began to feel as if it were breaking. I sensed her anger at God, her despair, her withered hopes and dreams. They all became my own.

I almost could not endure such a weight. But the next moment, when my eyes caught hers, I perceived a visible change taking place within her. The heaviness lifted. She wiped away her tears and a brightness returned to her face. Then, thanking me for listening, she set off with a lighter step for her car.

As she drove off and I returned to my own car, the weight on my shoulders overwhelmed me. In a sudden avalanche of intensity, sitting behind the wheel, I broke down and wept. All I could say was, "Christ Jesus, have mercy. Christ, have mercy. Christ, have mercy. Have mercy, O Lord, upon these Thy people!"

As I prayed, the weight gradually lifted. I knew that somehow, for a moment, I had shouldered with Jesus His cross, and through Him the pain of this mother. I had served as her intercessor, and as a result, Jesus had renewed her strength so that she could return once again to a debilitating and hopeless situation. Through me, I realized, God had worked a miracle.

As I sat in my car, overwhelmed by this experience, one of the elders, a simple man of profound faith who could have known nothing of what God had just done, came up to me and spoke these words:

"Pastor, for a long time I've felt like the Lord wanted me to tell you something. I never thought it was the right time. But tonight as I was praying for you, the Lord spoke clearly to me, and I have to obey. He said, *You must love us. Don't be so busy trying to change us; just love us. What we need is to be loved. Please just love us!*"

When I heard these words, part of me died. I realized I had completely missed the purpose of ministry. It is not to develop programs, start a new social revolution or get everybody filled with the Holy Spirit. Rather, it is to love with Christ's love. It is to love so much that we begin actually to live and die with others. When this happens, we discover the meaning of the Holy Spirit's power, for His power is His love in action.

The Power of Love

The only person who can really serve as healer, prophet or spiritual leader is one who loves people with Christ's love. Without that we may initiate good programs, make a lot of noise over social issues and preach fine biblical sermons, but all these activities will be spiritually empty. They do not mediate the transforming, liberating presence of Christ Jesus. In the wilderness all our programs may fail. We may find that we have none of the Spirit's power and gifts. But through the wilderness we learn what is essential: love. And it is in that love that we finally begin to show forth Christ's dynamic, mountain-moving power.

We are called not to those outward activities that are often used to define successful ministry. Rather we are called to the essential task of being a sacrament of the presence of God. Like Jesus we are to mediate God's presence to the world, and to carry the world to God. To enter this mystery of priesthood is to find in ourselves the same love that led Jesus to give up the throne of glory and exchange it for a cross. By such love as this, the world will know that we are Jesus' disciples, and they will know Jesus.

Only with love as our foundation will we be called to the many different forms of empowered ministry and service.

Questions for Reflection

1. What is God teaching you about love? Reflect on 1 Corinthians 13:2.
2. Make a list in your spiritual journal of the times you have experienced God's love in your life.
3. How are you being called beyond your own human capacity for love into Jesus' love for others?

11

There is no
distinction; since all
have sinned and fall
short of the glory
of God. . . .
Romans 3:22–23

Into
the Abyss
of Sin

At a global mission conference, while I was sitting at dinner, a friend of mine said to the person across the table, "Have you gotten in touch with that in yourself for which Christ had to die?" I remember nothing else he said, or even why he said it, but those words sank deep into my heart. For at that time I was not at all in touch with this reality. I did not know myself as a sinner.

Think about it for a moment. What is it about you that required Jesus Christ, the Son of God—from all eternity with God, God of gods, Light of lights, Creator and Ruler of the universe—to come down to earth and die a terrible death on a cross?

It is easy to think of many good reasons He should be crucified for the Nazis or the Japanese solders who committed unspeakable atrocities in Nanjing. It is obvious that they are sinners. But me? Do I really know myself as a sinner?

To know yourself as a sinner, to know why Christ had to die for you alone, is the secret of growing in relationship with Him.

If you do not know yourself this way, you will never understand the central mystery of the Christian faith: the Son of God bleeding and dying on a cross, then being raised from the dead. You will also never deeply know yourself.

To know ourselves truly, as God knows us, and to find ourselves as Christ finds us, is not within the reach of human faculties. It is a gift of revelation from the Holy Spirit. It is He who must open our hearts to show us the mystery of sin within us.

One of the purposes of the wilderness is to peel away our outer, protective layer of security that provides meaning, purpose and identity, that we may experience our soul's nakedness and that we may know the forces of darkness swirling in the depths of our own beings.

Such knowledge of ourselves is intolerable, however, unless we first know that we are loved and forgiven in Christ.

Forgiveness Precedes Judgment

Most likely Jesus could not have withstood the attacks of Satan in the wilderness if His heavenly Father's words, spoken at His baptism, had not been ringing in His soul: "This is my beloved Son, with whom I am well pleased" (Matthew 3:17). The assurance given by these words must have given Jesus the firmness of will to resist Satan. Likewise we, too, will never endure the wilderness unless we are first graced by a profound sense of God's love and acceptance. We must know that we stand upon the rock of His unshakable election. We must have engraved on our hearts that nothing in heaven or on earth can "separate us from the love of God in Christ Jesus our Lord" (Romans 8:38–39).

This is especially true when we look into the abyss of our own sin. Even to allow to consciousness the thought that we are unworthy, fit only to be cast into hell, is impossible unless we first know God's unfathomable love that accepts us even in this condition. Paul could know himself as the greatest of sinners only because he knew he was saved by absolutely no merit of his own, but only through faith in Jesus.

Those who do not know Christ cannot know themselves. They must hide behind their own imagined righteousness. The man or woman in Christ Jesus, however, knows that apart from Christ he or she has nothing, and is nothing, and so is wonderfully free to face his or her own shadows.

Knowledge of God's grace makes possible true knowledge of self. Yet only those who know their true condition can know the depth of God's love.

At the house of Simon, it was not the Pharisees resting complacently in their own self-righteousness who lavished love on Jesus. Rather it was the woman who had sinned much and been forgiven much, and therefore loved much (see Luke 7:36–50). When we look at our own wretched condition, and in contrast contemplate all that God has done for us in Christ, we are moved to a deeper love of our Lord.

In our spiritual journeys, wilderness times often follow experiences of God's grace. In the Old Testament it was the Exodus event that provided the people of Israel with concrete evidence of God's grace and election. This was a revelatory happening in that it displayed, in human history, God's nature and intentions for His people. The memory of their liberation from Egypt and passage into the Promised Land was to become the bedrock of their faith that would enable the Israelites to be faithful in times of testing. So it must be for us.

God may grant us such evidence in many ways. Perhaps an experience of being filled with the Holy Spirit assures us that the doctrines of the Christian faith are true, that Jesus Christ is real, that He really does love us and that He has called us. Or the assurance of God's grace and election may come through times of fruitful ministry or intense, loving fellowship. Whatever our experience, the firmest ground of all is the witness of Scripture. There, in Jesus Christ and in the witness of all the prophets, we can know God's gracious intentions for us.

It is this grounding in God's reality that prepares us for the wilderness. And in a paradoxical way, it is in the wilderness that this certainty is deepened.

Being Given Up to Sin

Years ago while in Korea, Joy Dawson, a leader of Youth With A Mission, told us at the Central Full Gospel Church in Seoul that if we were to grow as spiritual leaders, we must know ourselves as sinners. She urged us to pray that God would show us our sinfulness. To pray such a prayer is frightening but necessary. It is to say to God, "I want to see myself as You see me."

God shows us our sin in all sorts of ways. He has revealed my sin to me primarily through letting me experience it, and also by giving me clear visions of my sinful condition.

He usually preserves us from falling too deeply into sin. He guides us so that we are not tempted beyond what we can endure. But there are times in our lives, especially during the wilderness, when God withdraws His hand for a moment and gives us up to the sin within us, so we can experience our full depravity. How this happens is complex. There is surely collaboration among our own desires, the freedom of our will, the work of Satan and God withdrawing His protection.

Does it seem impossible that God would intentionally give us up to sin or to the torments of Satan for a season? He did so to Peter. He may, for His loving purposes, do it to you and me.

To be given up to one's sin is to have one's pride of self-righteousness shattered. Suddenly we find things in us that we are unable to control. And in the face of particular temptations, we are certain to fall.

Usually we come at sin with an attitude of arrogance: *Oh, sure, I can handle that. Nothing can threaten my integrity.* In this state of affairs we look with amazement or even contempt on those around us who have fallen. We may sneer at the *A* branded on the chest of the TV evangelist who committed adultery. We dismiss as impossible the racial hatred, cowardice, unfaithfulness, abuse of money or drinking problems of believers around us. We assume we really are superior. Our arrogance blinds us to the fact that we harbor within us the potential to commit the very same sins.

Was this not the attitude of Peter?

Peter said to Jesus, "Even though they all fall away, I will not."
And Jesus said to him, "Truly, I say to you, this very night, before
the cock crows twice, you will deny me three times." But he said
vehemently, "If I must die with you, I will not deny you." And
they all said the same.

Mark 14:29–31

Peter and the other disciples did not know themselves. So
for a while God gave them up to their sin. They denied Jesus
and fled. When the cock crowed, Peter broke down and wept.
Now he knew himself, and with this knowledge came the humility required for him to serve as leader of the early Church.
Although he had personal charisma and leadership ability, it
was the Holy Spirit who would accomplish things through him.
Apart from Christ he could do nothing but flee.

Another faithful servant whom God gave up to his sin was
King David. David was a man of great passion and power. He
loved the Lord with abandon. We see this in the way he threw
off all restraint and danced wildly before the Ark as it was carried into Jerusalem. He loved his son Absalom, who betrayed
him, with such devotion that it blinded him to the danger faced
by the kingdom. It is not surprising to find in a man of such
intensity and passion the tendency to lust, and it was to this sin
that David was given up.

David's temptation came at a time when he had enjoyed success after success. Under his leadership Israel had vanquished
her enemies. Now David had become so great that he no longer
had to lead his troops into battle but could remain at ease in
Jerusalem. This was his undoing.

It happened, late one afternoon, when David arose from his
couch and was walking upon the roof of the king's house, that
he saw from the roof a woman bathing; and the woman was very
beautiful.

2 Samuel 11:2

What a perfect setup! Like a chained tiger the king, who in the past had led his armies to battle, was staying home. Perhaps his success had made him a little less vigilant. Perhaps, too, having been anointed by the Lord with power and authority to establish Israel, he had begun to believe he was above the Law and the covenant. He could do anything he wanted and get away with it. But now the God who had protected David countless times, and given him the wisdom and courage to do what was right, withdrew His hand and gave David up to his sin. The king fell into lust so consuming that he was willing to kill one of his own faithful servants to satisfy it.

It took the words of the prophet Nathan to awaken David to his sin and bring him to repentance. Psalm 51 is testimony that David had been humbled and broken, that he knew his limits and his sin. It is always risky to guess the purposes of the Almighty, but perhaps the reason God let David fall into sin with Bathsheba was to keep him from falling into the hubris that has been the downfall of many great leaders and nations.

In the wilderness, God may give us up to our sin. He will shatter our arrogance and bring us to our knees to show us that we, too, are sinners and that we, too, have our limits beyond which we will fall.

The sin to which God may give you up will grow out of your own personality and circumstances. It may be anger, lust, fear, lying, spiritual pride, envy or something else. Look carefully at yourself and you will see the weak places in your integrity. Most likely it will be there that God withdraws His hand and lets the wall collapse.

Do not flatter yourself by thinking that your particular sin is of less consequence than that of someone else, which seems more obvious or destructive. Whatever your sin is, if it hinders the work of God and taints His glory, it is serious.

When God gives us up to sin, and if mercifully we are awakened, we must resist the temptation to pass responsibility for it to Satan, to others or to circumstances. These may be factors, of course, in why we have fallen, but the real source lies within us. The anger is ours. The lust, the envy, the hatred, the unfor-giveness—it is all ours. Our own sin has chained and bound us. If we are to grow, we must not hide behind excuses but accept who we are. God, by withdrawing His preserving hand for a moment, forces us to look into the abyss of our own sinfulness. If we do so, we will be sent crawling to the feet of Jesus, beg-ging for His mercy, praying that He will not leave us to our pal-try resources. Christ, and Christ alone, is the way of freedom.

Then, if we repent and turn again to our Lord, we may like David and Peter be restored to useful service. But if we remain unteachable and arrogant, He may withdraw His Holy Spirit's anointing and leave us behind, as the great work of God's King-dom flows on through others.

A word of warning: This is a dangerous subject, for we may be tempted to use these reflections about God giving us up to our sin as a way to condone falling into sin for spiritual growth! Do not be deceived. Although we may grow from such experi-ences, we will also have to suffer the consequences. Sin is odi-ous in the sight of God. And regardless of what good may come of it, we must reckon with the very real effects of sin and the judgment of God. King David repented and was humbled by the Bathsheba experience, yet God did not exempt him from the consequences of his sin. His first child by Bathsheba died and his home was cursed with lust, murder and rebellion. It will be the same for us, even though we also return and repent.

Pray that you will be humble enough to learn to know your-self and God without having to be given up to sin. For there is an easier way: the path of humble obedience.

Teach me your way, O LORD, and I will walk in your truth;
give me an undivided heart, that I may fear your name.

Psalm 86:11, NIV

Let God's law draw the lines past which you dare not go, and offer yourself quickly to Christ, that He may put to death in you all that is not pure and true.

Questions for Reflection

1. In your prayer journal, construct a history of God's grace toward you. Reflect on times when you have experienced His love, guidance, protection and forgiveness.
2. Reflect on an occasion when you were faced with temptation that you had no power to resist. What did you do? What did God do?
3. Have you ever been given up to sin?
4. What secret sin do you now carry in your heart?

12

He commanded us to
preach to the people
and to testify that
he is the one whom
God appointed as
judge of the living
and the dead.
Acts 10:42, NIV

Under
Judgment,
under Grace

God is love!

Yes, He certainly is, but make no mistake about the nature of His love. It is not mushy, insipid affection. His love embraces judgment as well as grace. It is commitment that takes ugly, unlovable, useless, sinful people and loves them to beauty and perfection.

Can you see Jesus amid the shouting of the mob, driving the moneychangers from the Temple? Where is the loving Lord who welcomed the little children into His arms? Right there with a whip in His hand! His love is a purifying love, which includes judgment as well as forgiveness. In the wilderness we experience both forms of Jesus' love.

We shrink at the idea of God's judgment. It is more pleasant to talk about grace and love. After all, we want to attract others to Jesus, not scare them away! But to know the mystery of sin within us is to know the fierceness of God's judgment against that sin. And further on in the darkness, if we plumb the depths of His wrath and judgment, we discover His love once again. While we are under judgment, however, it does not feel like love, only annihilation.

While I was on an eight-day silent Jesuit retreat, the Lord gave me a series of visions, three of which I will share in this chapter. They came while I was praying with the Scriptures, providing a terrifying firsthand experience of God's judgment, and finally of His salvation.

Before I describe them, some observations are in order regarding the nature of the retreat I made. A review of one's sin is not something to be undertaken lightly. Do so only at the clear leading of the Holy Spirit; otherwise it may prove a fruitless exercise in introverted masochism. Also, do not take such a journey backward into your sin alone. It may be more than you can bear. Like Jesus, who took Peter, James and John with Him into the Garden of Gethsemane, do so in the presence of friends (preferably wakeful ones!). You will need them for support and in order to help you keep perspective. They will also assist you in discerning the validity of the images or feelings that may sweep over you. You may also need them to believe for you, when you lose all faith, that God can forgive you.

I could not have walked this road alone and thankfully did not have to. There was my wife, whose love and support were always present. There was the spiritual director, a priest who worked with me to discern every movement of the Spirit and helped me sort it out. There was the rest of the community of fellow travelers who, although bound to silence, embraced and sustained me in this troubled journey in numerous wordless ways—a smile, a twinkle in the eye, a hand lovingly placed upon my shoulder.

The retreat itself was a wilderness within the wilderness, the lowest point in two years of desolation, while I was in the parish. On the retreat I met God and was shattered. I believe it completed God's intentions for taking me into the wilderness in the first place and marked the transition into a new calling, to the

113

mission field. The geographic location was the Jesuit retreat center, but the battle took place in the realm of the spirit. It was the final struggle with myself and my decisive conflict with God.

The only language I can use to communicate what happened is that of dreams, visions and words from Scripture. The visions will, I hope, give you more insight into the dynamic of spiritual wilderness.

Were they real? Unlike my encounter with Satan in the field, they took place not outside of me but in my imagination—a faculty that, when directed by the Holy Spirit, may be the door through which we walk into objective spiritual reality. Were these internal spiritual events really encounters with God? The answer to this question must, like all valid religious experience, be based on four criteria: Do they give glory to Jesus Christ? Are they consistent with Scripture? Are they witnessed to by others filled with the Holy Spirit? And do they yield positive and objectively verifiable results?

I invite you to judge for yourself.

Compiling a History of Sin

Each day of the silent Jesuit retreat, the priest who served as my spiritual director gave me a prayer request and some Scripture to guide my praying, based on what together we thought the Spirit of God was doing within me.

One day my prayer was to know the mystery of sin within me. The Scripture I was given was Romans 1:18–32, about how God gives people up to their sin, and Matthew 25, about the Last Judgment. According to the spiritual exercises of Ignatius, I was first to write a history of my sinfulness:

> First point. This is the record of my sins. I will call to mind all the sins of my life, reviewing year by year and period by period. Three things will help me in this: first, to consider the place where I live; secondly, my dealings with others; thirdly, the office I have held. . . .[1]

I set about this exercise with a great deal of reluctance. No one takes pleasure in reviewing his sins. As I entered the chapel and asked God to show me my sins, I did not have long to wait before a Pandora's box was opened. Many long-forgotten sins began to play like a movie before the eyes of my imagination. The events returned to me in all their sordid detail—times when I lusted, hated and refused to forgive. Instance after instance of disobedience and rebellion against the clear leading of the Holy Spirit. He showed me how others would have been brought closer to Him had I only obeyed Him. To see the thwarting or delay of God's redeeming work in others because of my failure to obey was an awful torment.

In all that procession of sins, however, my lack of compassion toward others returned with ferocious intensity and cut most deeply into my heart.

I remembered something that had happened when I was in South Vietnam. My father had been on assignment with the U.S. Embassy in Saigon and I was there for the summer between college and seminary working with an American adoption agency. I recalled walking from the Embassy swimming pool to my father's apartment—a short walk of four or five blocks. Four years later I could almost feel the balmy, humid night, hear the sounds and smell the smells of that tragic city.

Suddenly, out of the anonymous flow of traffic, a rickshaw pulled up in front of me. The driver's drawn, haggard body seemed but a barely clothed skeleton perched precariously on the seat. In his face and eyes I detected the look of smothered despair and heart-rending sadness—the fruit of hunger and unrelenting labor. His countenance was momentarily lifted, however, by the hope of a customer. In broken English he offered his services.

I had money in my pocket and could get my exercise some other way. I saw the poor man's need, his desperation. And within my heart I sensed the urging of the Holy Spirit to reach out to him in compassion and offer him work. I saw and felt all that, but I did not care.

"No," I said blithely, stepping up my pace.

I looked away, but not before I saw the man's countenance fall. Slowly, with painful weariness, he turned and disappeared again into the traffic.

Then I stopped on the sidewalk, jerked out of the myopia of my own self-centeredness. I knew that this man, and perhaps a family, would know the pangs of hunger that night. And I knew that I had sinned.

In the ongoing vision of my sinfulness, the rickshaw driver's face danced among all the specters, his eyes of sadness indicting me. They became the eyes of the One to whom I had refused a cup of cool water. His eyes became the eyes of all those I had failed, or to whom I had refused to show compassion. All these individuals were "the least of these My brothers," and now they rose up, a great host of judges with eyes like flames, to condemn me.

I fled from this vision and tried to present to my judges the occasions when I had shown compassion. But the Spirit, who discerns the hidden things of the heart, stripped away my pretense to reveal the vile motives behind even those acts of compassion. It had been out of pride, fear or desire for personal glory that I had reached out in kindness. There was no purity in me! I had sinned in my worst deeds as well as in my best, for that is our wretched, fallen condition.

By the time I reached the present in my history of sinfulness, I had compiled a seven-page litany of confessed sins. The Spirit released me and I left the chapel for a walk, feeling slightly sick to my stomach. A deep, wordless sorrow had begun to infuse my whole being. As I walked about the grounds, where previously I had found comfort and pleasure, her charms were now hidden from a sinner such as I.

Meditating on Two Thieves

In the evening I returned to the large chapel where I had first encountered the silence of God. I was in the oratory—a little balcony high up in the back of the sanctuary, above the choir loft. At this great height I could look directly across the chapel at a large fresco of the crucifixion painted on the wall behind the altar. The high, vaulted ceiling magnified the space and added to its majesty and mystery.

As I started to pray, a sense of the holy presence of God filled me. I lifted to Him the request to know my sinfulness. "Father, I am in a terrible situation, for I am sick, yet I do not know the extent of my sickness. I do not even know that I need to ask and receive Thy healing medicine. Reveal my sickness unto me, I pray Thee, in Thy mercy."

God led me to read Scriptures concerning the crucifixion:

One of the criminals who were hanged railed at him, saying, "Are you not the Christ? Save yourself and us!" But the other rebuked him, saying, "Do you not fear God, since you are under the same sentence of condemnation? And we indeed justly; for we are receiving the due reward of our deeds; but this man has done nothing wrong." And he said, "Jesus, remember me when you come into your Kingdom." And he said to him, "Truly, I say to you, today you will be with me in Paradise."

Luke 23:39–43

As I prayed, I looked intently at the fresco. In the center was Jesus on the cross, blood dripping from His hands, the agony of death in His face. On either side were the two thieves.

Suddenly there occurred a shift of perspective, and I saw the scene as I had not seen it before. My eyes left the image of the crucified Christ and focused on the two crucified thieves. The tortured, dying forms of those condemned men captivated me.

As I reflected on them, I realized that the one who had mocked Jesus bore, in this fresco, the look of death. Not just physically had he been overcome by death, but the brush of the artist had made the body transparent, revealing his spirit to be dead as well. My eyes shifted to the other thief. He, too, was caught in the grip of death and his body was nearly dead,

117

yet the same masterstroke of the artist had caught his spirit, and he was alive. His was life in the midst of death.

This painting, I realized, was a depiction of us all. All humanity is dying because of sin that severs us from the life of God. Each of us is a fallen creature out of whom only evil deceits and blasphemies issue. Every one of us is bound securely to a cross of sin and death. This is our inheritance from Adam.

Just like the two thieves, there stands in the midst of humankind a twofold division. There are those who, by the grace of God, know their guilt and the nature of the cross on which they are fixed, but who turn to Jesus and ask to be remembered in His Kingdom. This is the way of life even in the midst of death. Then there are those who do not know their plight and who mock Christ. Theirs is death in death.

The moment this insight flashed into my awareness, it was transformed into a question addressed personally to me: *Where are you? You, too, are upon your well-deserved cross. You, too, are dying. Which thief are you—the one on the right or the left?*

I shuddered at the chasm between life and death that had just opened up before me.

Contemplating Judgment and God's Wrath

To know one's sin is one thing. But this awareness is in itself incomplete. Sin is defined by relationship. There is a Being against whom we have sinned. It is in the presence of God's light, justice and love that the black shadow of our sin is cast. It is His standard, His law, that we have broken, His work and glory that have been hindered and tainted. Thus, to begin to experience one's sin is also to experience the judgment and wrath of God.

For this hour of prayer, I came not to the high chapel's oratory, with its brooding mystery and fresco of the Passion, but to what was called the Holy Spirit chapel—a small, cozy room with a large, bright tapestry of the Holy Spirit as a descending dove.

118

The final visions occurred in a time of prayer on Matthew 25:31–46:

"When the Son of man comes in his glory, and all the angels with him, then he will sit on his glorious throne. Before him will be gathered all the nations, and he will separate them one from another as a shepherd separates the sheep from the goats, and he will place the sheep at his right hand, but the goats at the left. . . .'Truly, I say to you, as you did it to one of the least of these my brethren, you did it to me.' . . . And they will go away into eternal punishment, but the righteous into eternal life."

Matthew 25:31–33, 40, 46

These words of Jesus held my attention in sweet embrace and transported me into the realm of the Spirit. The image of Christ dividing the sheep from the goats grew vivid. In a subtle shift of consciousness, the barrier between the objective and subjective fell away and I entered the reality of the biblical images.

I found myself in the Last Judgment. All was fire and light. Before me stood the cross in stark profile against an azure sky. On the cross hung the crucified but risen and exalted Jesus. I was among the vast multitude about to be judged. As each person's turn came to stand before the cross, Jesus asked one question only: "Have you done it unto the least of these, My brethren?"

As I waited my turn, my thoughts were swirling. I knew I could not stand before Him guiltless. What was I to do or say?

Suddenly, superimposed over this vision, I was given another picture—a vision within a vision, as one may dream that he is dreaming. In this second vision I stood among a great multitude about to be judged, except this judgment was of the sort that took place in Nazi death camps. Black smoke billowed into the pallid sky. My nostrils burned with the stench of burning flesh. All about were screams of anguish. Before us stood our judge, an SS officer with eyes of steel. With a careless flick of his wrist, he sent some to an asphyxiating death in the gas ovens, and others to the slow torture of being worked to death.

As I waited for my time to be judged, I was filled with horror and despair.

Just as I stepped forward, in a shift of consciousness given as an act of God's grace, I found myself standing not before the merciless SS officer, but before Jesus.

He asked me in a voice of infinite tenderness, as Creator to creation, as loving father to child, "My son, what have you done for the least of these, My brethren?"

As I stood before Him, I began to tremble, for I had to confess that I had done very little. As I lifted before Him my paltry store of good deeds, I knew that nothing I had done or ever could do was sufficient to save me. So overcome was I by emotion that I fell from my chair onto the floor and pleaded, "Mercy, Lord, mercy! Jesus Christ, Son of the living God, have mercy on me, a sinner."

As I prayed, a voice of judgment thundered, "Not only have you not done it unto the least of these, but you have also lusted. Not only have you lusted, but you have also been prideful. Not only have you been arrogant, but you have also held your anger past the setting of the sun."

Each word evoked the remembrance of my sins and fell on me like a sledgehammer. With each pounding blow, I knew I deserved to be damned and destined for wrathful oblivion. Then I was overwhelmed with blackness.

I lay on the floor a long time. Gradually I lifted my face and saw above me the tapestry of the descending dove, the life-giving Holy Spirit. Through the eyes of the Spirit, I saw that I lay at the foot of the cross. I knew, as I had never known before, that Jesus Christ is the rock of my salvation. He is my hope, my life and my all.

Late that night I returned to the large chapel where I had first experienced the silence of God's presence. It was dark but for the flickering paschal candle. An icy wind buffeted about outside, rattling the stained glass windows and stirring up an occasional cold draft. In the dark, windy silence, beyond all thoughts and words, I was aware of God's presence—the outskirts, the dimmest rays, of His brilliant, omnipotent and majestic being. He was there!

I had come with petitions, but these died within me when I considered my unworthiness to receive anything from Him. So I sat wordlessly in His presence, which was indescribably sweet.

I share these images of my sin and God's judgment and mercy because they describe not only my condition, but the condition of us all. We are sinners in whom there is no righteousness. God may take us into the wilderness, with all its pain, to teach us precisely this. His aim is to get us to lose all confidence in ourselves, so that in humility we turn to Jesus Christ.

As we discover our true nature as sinners fit only for eternal hell, Jesus impresses His reality on each of us by saying to our lostness, "I am the way, and the truth, and the life; no one comes to the Father, but by me" (John 14:6). In Him are all good things, our righteousness, our very lives. Outside Him is death and nothingness.

Questions for Reflection

1. Have you gotten in touch with that in yourself for which Jesus Christ had to die?
2. Write a history of your sin, if the Holy Spirit guides you to do so. It may be helpful to use Ignatius' guideline as you do this: "I will call to mind all the sins of my life, reviewing year by year and period by period. Three things will help me in this: first, to consider the place where I live; secondly, my dealings with others; thirdly, the office I have held."
3. Consider planning a spiritual retreat.
4. Ponder now the extent of God's grace toward you. Meditate on John 3:16.
5. Have you really met Jesus Christ?

Part *four*

Encounter
with God

13

At a lodging place on the way the LORD met [Moses] and sought to kill him. Then Zipporah took a flint and cut off her son's foreskin, and touched Moses' feet with it, and said, "Surely you are a bridegroom of blood to me!" So he let him alone.

Exodus 4:24–26

God Is Out to Kill Us

In the wilderness we have struggled with the devil and with ourselves. But our final struggle—the one that underlies all the others—is with God. It takes place in the deepest regions of our souls, in realms that have no words, so to talk about this battle, we are reduced to poetry and to symbols.

The story of the Lord seeking to kill Moses is a strange one. Why would God try to kill His chosen servant? Why did Moses' wife have to save him? If Zipporah had not cut off their son's foreskin, the sign of God's own covenant, would Moses actually have been slain? What, then, of God's plan to liberate His people? A God who would slay His servant seems as unnatural as a mother who would kill her own child. Yet it was God the Father who allowed His only begotten Son to be crucified.

Moses had failed to circumcise his son. This was a breach of the fundamental covenant between God and the Hebrews. So God lashed out at Moses in righteous anger. Zipporah, Moses' intercessor, kept the covenant on Moses' behalf, so God let him live. This was to teach Moses, and us as well, that God's chosen servants are not exempt from the requirements of His covenant. They, too, must obey God's law. Perhaps through this experience Moses learned another lesson: the real person to fear was not Pharaoh but God Himself.

I do not know whether the following observation is actually so, or whether it is simply my projection, but in the wilderness our real adversary seems to be God, who is out to undo us.

God is the Author of all things; even the devil is under His power. Is it not the Lord who sets up circumstances? Did He not create us with our human nature? In the wilderness it is as if all other spheres—our struggles with the devil, with others, with organizations, with ourselves—fall to the wayside, leaving a single arena of conflict: us against God. God compels us to face Him alone. Then He throws down the gauntlet: *My will or yours?* We look for escape but find no way out because He is the omnipotent Lord.

We may seek to avoid this last arena by fleeing His presence. We may plunge to the depths of our own sin or climb to the heights of our own success, only to find that He has set us up, driven us into a corner. Again and again he says, *My will or yours?* It is absurd to fight; but don't we, against all odds, take the challenge?

So, yes, He must kill us! He must nail us to the cross, just as He allowed His own Son to be crucified. I can see Him, loving Father that He is, with tears streaming down His face but with iron determination and ferocious love, taking the spikes in His own hand and pounding them through ours, that we may die.

Perhaps God's flaming love would totally annihilate us, except for those who, like Zipporah, rush to our rescue. They intercede for us, call us away from our sin and love us—anything to defend us against the certain destruction toward which our battle with God is taking us. They remind God of His own covenant and plead with Him to hold back His hand, that we may be saved.

Even so, let us set one fact in our minds: God is out to kill us. He wants to put to death all that is not of Him, all that is not holy and pure. And we must die before we can experience the newness of the resurrection, before we can be of much use in the Kingdom of God. We must perish before we can begin to live, before we can receive and use the power and gifts of the Holy Spirit for the glory of God. Jesus says to each of us, "Take up your cross and follow Me." Never forget that the cross is an instrument of death—*our* death!

These are strange and terrible thoughts, I know. They grow out of the wilderness, where neat theological syntheses collapse. There we experience the raw paradoxes and mysteries of our faith—God's love and wrath, our freedom of will and His sovereignty. We also face the mysteries of good and evil, of prayer and of the crucified God. I stand in awe of such truths and offer nothing but silence to explain them. Yet I can affirm out of the wilderness that they are not empty dogmas but descriptions of the very core of reality, and the only adequate interpretation of our deepest experience.

Christian Leaders Are under God's Law

God sought to kill Moses because, although he was called to be a leader in the covenant reality, he was not living in that reality. The great temptation of spiritual leadership is for the leader to believe he or she is above God's law. This is an abuse of spiritual power. Indeed, it is the way of great evil. God will either kill this tendency in us or remove us from spiritual leadership.

The story of Samson stands as a warning to every Holy Spirit–empowered servant of God. As long as this judge lived the vows he had made to God, he had the Spirit upon him for mighty acts. But his character was depraved. He was unrestrained in his sexual desires and ruthless in his revenge. He seemed to feel that his anointing gave him license to do anything he wanted. This attitude led him to fall in love with Philistine women. His parents objected, but driven by unrestrained

127

lust and allowed by the mysterious providence of God, he went forward with one relationship after another. This put him outside the protection of God's covenant and into the hands of the enemies of Israel.

The frightening paradox of Samson's sin was that God seems to have allowed it so He could work judgment and mayhem on the Philistines. At last, however, Samson, through God and his own sin, was placed in the hands of a woman whose seductions and nagging he could not endure. When he broke covenant by revealing to Delilah the secret of his strength, God withdrew the power of the Holy Spirit from him, and Samson was captured and humiliated. God did give him one last burst of power to avenge his blindness, but he was crushed along with the Philistines.

The story of Samson haunted me in the wilderness. My great terror was that I would be tested beyond what I could endure, and fall into sin. God would kill me, first by withdrawing His anointing, then by setting me aside from His work. I knew in a deep, inexplicable way that if I did step over the lines of God's call and covenant, physical and spiritual death awaited me as His judgment. Yet during my battle in the wilderness, I was driven against all wisdom to test the limits and believe the delusion that because I had the Holy Spirit upon me, I was free to sin.

The temptations for us to step beyond the defining lines of our covenant relationship with God are sometimes subtle, at other times blatant. Their exact nature is unique to each of us and depends on the structures of our personalities. I will not catalog sins here. Rather, go gaze at your reflection in the mirror of Scripture and you will clearly see those places in the protective walls of God's covenant that you will be tempted—no, driven!—to breach.

I have clung desperately to two intercessors who have stood as my Zipporah. They pleaded my case before God, had faith for me when I lost all faith and held me accountable, lovingly but ruthlessly, to the law and calling of God. Without their interventions, I know I would have been destroyed.

In the wilderness, in the battle of opposing wills, an anointed leader like Moses either surrenders to the will of God and submits to His law, or else the anointing is lifted. If leaders let the wilderness accomplish its work of killing their egos and moving them to die to themselves, they will continue in power and leadership. If not, God will remove them.

No one on earth is more wretched and tragic than a person called to spiritual leadership and empowered by the Holy Spirit who has then fallen into sin and been set aside from God's great Kingdom purposes.

A Battle to the Death

Throughout each of my wilderness experiences, I was tempted to cross the line into what I knew would result in the loss of the Holy Spirit's power. The deeper battles of the wilderness, however, were not with particular sins, but with my will against God's. To surrender my will was life. To fight Him to the end, I knew, was truly death.

One such battle marked the final phase of an extended time in the wilderness and the transition into the next phase of peace and fruitfulness.

Laura and I, as missionaries in Taiwan, were involved in a wave of Holy Sprit renewal that was igniting Presbyterian churches in Taiwan and Korea. Everything was going extremely well. I assumed we were called to the mission field long term. Driven by a soul-deep restlessness, however (which I now recognize as part of my midlife crisis), I went to Korea in December 1988 for a week of prayer at Jesus Abbey, the Anglican charismatic prayer community, assuming God would affirm my dreams of building a prayer center in Taiwan for the evangelization of China.

While I was up on top of a mountain, wrestling with God for direction, the Holy Spirit fell on me. I had a glorious sense of Jesus being right there with me, embracing me, loving me and forgiving me.

Suddenly an image of a map of Taiwan burst into my mind. It was composed of a collage of faces. Then the map expanded to include the rest of Asia. Then it exploded in quantum leaps to include North and South America, and then Africa, until it embraced the whole world.

With this image came a word that addressed my whole being: *You are not to rest in Taiwan. Rather, I am calling you to an international ministry of renewal for the advancement of my Kingdom worldwide.*

I was astonished and overwhelmed. I knew I had met Jesus on this mountain, for my heart still burned within me and the fragrance of His presence lingered about me. But I could not believe I had heard the call right.

When I got back to Taiwan, I told no one other than Laura and a trusted friend about the vision. We prayed and waited.

Two weeks later I received a letter from a man I had met only once for about ten minutes. Brick Bradford, general secretary of Presbyterian and Reformed Renewal Ministries, wrote that two weeks before at a board meeting, as they had prayed, they had felt the Lord saying that I was the one called to replace him. Was I willing to leave Taiwan and begin work on January 1, 1990?

This organization appeared to offer a suitable vehicle for me to express the calling I received on the mountain. But this calling, and the open door to walk toward it, were like a whip that put me into combat with the Creator of the universe. I had sick images of myself as a Roman gladiator, driven by blows into an arena already littered with the mangled bodies of failed ministers, to face God as my invincible foe.

Everything in me wanted to accept this call because I knew it was right for me. At the same time, paradoxically, everything in me rebelled against accepting it, because I knew that answering such a call was impossible without total dependence on the Holy Spirit. This truly was a mission impossible, designed so that only God would get the glory. So my ego rebelled. I fought God.

Nevertheless I obeyed. In the summer of 1989 Laura and I left Taiwan and returned to the United States. We settled in

Montreat, North Carolina, for the six months before moving to Oklahoma, where the office of PRRMI was then located. All the while I resisted this call. My family and body returned to the States, but not my heart. It was still clinging to my missionary identity and ministry in Taiwan.

The final battle took place the day before I was to appear before the PRRMI board of directors for formal approval as executive director. On that August day I wrestled with many issues about accepting the position. These came in the form of two vivid prayer visions warning me of the blessings, and also of the challenges, that lay ahead.

First I saw myself in the robes of a prophet standing in front of a vast crowd of people from all nations. I stood helpless, not knowing what to do. Then I was aware of the moving of the Holy Spirit like a fragrant breeze, blowing through the crowd and bringing a wild, dancing melody. I stood petrified, not knowing how to respond. Then God commanded, *Dance! Dance with the Spirit!* Awkwardly I obeyed and started to dance. For what seemed an eternity, the crowd stared, unmoved. Suddenly one person leaped up and joined the dance. Then another, and another, until the vision expanded. It was the great Marriage Feast of the Lamb, and people from all nations were dancing in the presence of Jesus.

What I feared, I realized from this prayer vision, was lonely obedience and having nothing within me that could move people or accomplish God's work of renewing the Church and reaching the world for Jesus. All I could do was, in faith, obey the leading of the Holy Spirit, and God would do the rest. But I fought this call to helpless dependence on God and the necessity of radical obedience.

The second vision was worse. In it I was wearing a business suit and carrying a briefcase full of plans and projects relating to Church renewal and world evangelization. But snarling gray wolves were leaping at me all around. I was terrified and wanted a safe place in which to hide. Then came the command, *Walk forward. Walk out the vision I have given you and trust My provision and protection.*

I knew the wolves portrayed the ferocious spiritual warfare that lay ahead as Satan tried to block the fulfillment of God's vision. Still, terrified of moving forward, I only wanted to find a secure hiding place. I knew the battle would cost me everything, perhaps even my life.

So I fought God. The issue was simple and terrible: His will or mine? I knew He wanted me to die. My ego, my will, my dreams—everything in me rose up in rebellion. At the same time I knew there would be no joy, no peace, no life outside His will. Besides, this looked like the invitation to a great adventure, not only in the realm of the Spirit but around the world. I knew, too, that if I did not die to self, I really *would* die.

So one night I phoned Harris Ricks, the fellow who had walked with me in the cemetery. Ever since junior high school Harris and I had wrestled with God alongside one another. We met Jesus together. In college I stood by him as he struggled with accepting the call to the ministry. Year after year we had helped each other be faithful to God's calling on our lives.

One summer night, for example, when he was serving his first church and I was in my wilderness in my church, we had gone for a long walk out in the country. We had just seen a presentation of the Shroud of Turin, the medieval relic that may have been Jesus' burial cloth. On this ancient cloth is the imprint and blood of a man who had been crucified. Harris and I were discussing the scientific report of the shroud and, most of all, wondering what Jesus was really like.

Suddenly Harris said, "You know, if the image on that cloth really is Jesus, He was around five feet eleven inches tall. How tall are you?"

"Five eleven and a half."

"Yes, just about the same height as Jesus."

Suddenly Jesus was there walking with us. He was invisible, but I knew within my being that He had joined us and was walking with us.

At that moment Harris gripped my arm and whispered, "He's here!"

In myself came the question, birthed from beyond me, *Lord, what do You want us to do?* But what I spoke was an astonished, "What do we do?"

Harris answered, "Just keep walking!"

I believe with my whole heart that at that moment, Jesus spoke in the words of my friend: *Just keep walking. Walk with me. Walk in the path I have set before you.*

So we walked in the balmy summer night filled with the sound of crickets and the fragrance of honeysuckle. And for about a mile the resurrected Jesus walked with us. There was no need for words, worship, prayer or anything else. He simply graced us with His presence.

After the presence lifted, we walked late into the night, too filled with joy and wonder to stop.

So on my night of battle with God, I needed my brother as the one through whom Jesus had said, *Just keep walking.* Because that night I wanted desperately to turn back. I also needed Harris as an intercessor who, like Zipporah, would stand between God and me.

That night was my Gethsemane. On a mountain in Montreat, beside a stream, I fought with God. His will or mine? After hours of struggle, and in the realm of the Spirit, with Harris, my intercessor, standing silently beside me, I broke inside. God killed my will and my rebellion. I died! Finally I was able with a whole heart to say, "O.K., Lord, I obey. I will accept this call and walk out the vision You have given . . . regardless of the cost."

I was flooded with joy and peace, and there was given me the gift of faith to count on God for supernatural provision and direction.

Killed by the Flaming Presence of God

If you are in the wilderness and locked in a combat of wills, the only hope I can offer is for you to die quickly! Let God kill you. Surrender your will to Him. In the battle it seems like stepping into an abyss—the most outrageous, irrational action you can possibly take. It will not only seem like death, but it *will* be. Afterward, however, a strange thing will happen. God will not only bless you with life eternal and overflowing, but your will, freedom and joy will now all be submitted to serving Him. To win against God and not to let Him kill you is the way of true and certain death. So choose life!

One other word of advice, born in the barrenness of the wilderness: Take a friend with you as your intercessor. Remember the stories of Moses and Jesus. They were not alone in their battles. If you are, most likely you will lose.

I know none of this makes any logical sense. It is harsh and terrible. It is, however, the very heart of following Jesus Christ. God puts all those He loves through this struggle to the death.

Jesus was crucified after a night battle in the Garden of Gethsemane in which He finally said, "Father, not My will but Thine be done." The next day His cry from the cross, "Into Thy hands I commend My spirit," was the working out of the death He had already died when He surrendered His will in the Garden.

The apostle Paul presented this terrible road of death as the way for all of us:

> I have been crucified with Christ and I no longer live, but Christ lives in me. The life I live in the body, I live by faith in the Son of God, who loved me and gave himself for me.
>
> Galatians 2:20, NIV

These familiar words are calmly and triumphantly written. But behind them, what combat of opposing wills did Paul endure? Only those who have been killed in the wilderness can grasp their full meaning.

You know that your wilderness journey is almost over when joyfully, from your own experience, Paul's words become yours.

How does God kill us? By His presence! Each wilderness period I have undergone has been difficult in its own way, but one characteristic is common to all: I experienced an intense engagement with God. At times He was absent and silent, at other times powerfully and mystically present. But I realize now that even in His apparent absence, He was profoundly present. Even while rebelling against God, I was confirming His hold on me.

It may be that wilderness is not a time of the withdrawal of the presence of God, but the time when we are drawn by His mysterious love into a closer orbit. The fiery love becomes too hot, His demands more than we can bear. Once we have died, He releases us to a more comfortable distance. There we carry on, attuned to His will, aware of His presence, yet not overwhelmed by His majesty or locked in a mortal combat of warring wills. It is still true that no one can look at God and live. In the wilderness God lets us see a little of Him, then returns us to a more comfortable blindness.

The purpose of all this pain and struggle: to bring us into God, that we may be His and His alone. To achieve this end, God did not spare even His own Son—nor will He spare us.

Questions for Reflection

1. Have you ever felt God was trying to kill you? How?
2. Where has Satan tempted you to think that because you have been moving in the power and gifts of the Holy Spirit, you are above God's law?
3. What is it in you that God is trying to put to death?

O Lᴏʀᴅ, thou hast deceived me, and I was deceived; thou art stronger than I, and thou hast prevailed. I have become a laughingstock all the day; every one mocks me. For whenever I speak, I cry out, I shout, "Violence and destruction!" For the word of the Lᴏʀᴅ has become for me a reproach and derision all day long. If I say, "I will not mention him, or speak any more in his name," there is in my heart as it were a burning fire shut up in my bones, and I am weary with holding it in, and I cannot.
Jeremiah 20:7–9

14

Anger at God

Jeremiah's joy and consolation were God and the word of God that he was compelled to speak. "Thy words were found," he wrote, "and I ate them, and thy words became to me a joy and the delight of my heart; for I am called by thy name, O Lᴏʀᴅ, God of hosts" (Jeremiah 15:16). But Jeremiah seemed to grow bitter against God. Long obedience to the prophetic task of proclaiming judgment against the people of Israel sent him into a wilderness. He was filled with anger and pain. Forbidden to marry, he was left out of the common pleasures of life. While others rejoiced, he had to sit alone brooding with his message of judgment. Apparently he stopped experiencing the joy of God's word and the sustaining presence of God. For he cried out to God, "Why is my pain unceasing, my wound incurable, refusing to be healed? Wilt thou be to me like a deceitful brook, like waters that fail?" (verse 18).

For the sake of the prophetic task, Jeremiah had given up everything and had looked to God for full support. Now even that had dried up! Later he cried out in anger, "O LORD, thou hast deceived me, and I was deceived" (Jeremiah 20:7). He wanted to abandon the prophetic task and no longer relentlessly speak God's judgment. No more did he take joy and delight in the word of God. It had become like fire in his bones with neither joy nor sweetness.

Our Natural Response

Our natural response to God, like Jeremiah's, as we encounter Him in the wilderness, is love mingled with hatred, praise tainted by anger. It is His Spirit who drives us there, after all, and only with His permission is Satan able to torment us. At heart it is God with whom we have to deal. He is the One who gave us a tremendous experience of being filled with the Holy Spirit or granted us effective ministry, and it is He who has now withdrawn His Spirit's empowering. So if we are to be angry, let's be angry with the right Person—God!

In my own wilderness, I boiled with anger at my situation, at those around me and at myself. But when I looked deeply enough into the blackness in my spirit, I found that the real object of my anger was God. During this time the words of Jeremiah became my words: "God, You deceived me!"

My rage against God found many expressions, but as a result it drove me from Him. I did not want to pray, nor did I want to obey Him. On many occasions I was ready to give up being a pastor as well as a Christian.

"God, I've had enough of Your persistent call to perfection! Why not just give myself up to my sin? Why should I carry such a cross, when no one else seems to have such a burden? To hell with Your will! I'll do it my way."

And, "God, this is Your work, Your ministry and Your people. If You're not going to do anything, why the hell should I?"

During one of my worst times of wilderness, I was so filled with anger at God that for weeks I could not pray. I hated Him, I hated the Church, I hated being a Christian and I hated myself.

Whenever I came to prayer, a dull blackness seemed to fill me with confusion, blotting out all communication.

One night I was so tormented with anger at God that sleep was impossible. Finally, around two in the morning, I leaped out of bed with an oath, disturbing Laura, got dressed and went outside. I started walking down the desolate country roads made brilliant by the light of a full moon. Knowing that only through restored communion with God would I find peace, I tried to pray. But, consumed with blackness, I was unable say a word. The angry dullness blocked all lines of communication. I could not even shout or curse at Him.

I must have walked five miles in this state. Suddenly I felt my tongue begin to flutter. I became conscious of a Presence moving with me as I walked, and I knew I was no longer alone. The Holy Spirit was ready to bring light into my darkness and restore order to my chaos.

At that moment I realized abruptly that I was being provided a choice. I could decide whether to let the anger continue to consume me by quenching the gentle stirring of the Spirit, or I could open myself and allow the Spirit to do His work.

I hesitated a moment, then let the gift of tongues come. With it I was able to pray again, and in my prayer I poured out my anger, hurt and despair. I expressed it all to Him. Slowly the blackness lifted, and I was able to praise and thank God for His abundant mercy and love.

My situation remained unaltered, of course, but my relationship with my Maker had changed. That often opens the way for a change in circumstances.

The Right Response

So what do we do with the anger that may seethe within us against God during the wilderness? We must express it to Him.

Many Christians feel it is not Christian to have angry feelings at God, so they suppress them. They do not admit that they really hate or mistrust God, and they walk around with a mask of sweet piety, while inside holding a great store of resentment toward their Creator. Often they express this resentment instead toward the church, toward the minister or toward someone else in God's service.

Anger, if left too long in our hearts, settles deep in our unconscious minds. Like ice in our hearts, it causes us to lose all joy in our salvation. Nature loses its beauty and human relationships their warmth.

Take a lesson from Jeremiah. He expressed his anger to God. In prayer we should do the same. Shout at Him! Let all your bitterness come pouring out. We do not need to be afraid; God's love is vast enough to accept us. He can take it.

Satan tempts us to hold in our anger: *Oh, it's not Christian to have such thoughts.* He holds out to us a false ideal of Christianity that says we must become inhuman. But Christ enables us to become fully human, and that includes our feelings.

Who of us when we were young did not hate our earthly parents when they disciplined us or made us do difficult but necessary things? Likewise it is natural that we should at times feel anger or even hatred toward God, our heavenly parent. The anger we experience toward Him is a natural symptom of being hurt, like the pain we feel when we touch something hot. Anger is a cry of alarm, telling us we are being hurt. Anger means that things precious to us—like our preconceptions, our desires, our loves or our egos—are being threatened by God. The cross hurts! If we do not feel anger, we are not being authentic to the situation. To cover up this pain with a sweet smile of Christian piety is to create a false religion and to deny the reality of Christ's crucifixion.

After Jeremiah expressed his struggle with anger, sense of deception and abandonment to God, he received an answer:

> Therefore, thus says the LORD: "If you return, I will restore you, and you shall stand before me. If you utter what is precious, and not what is worthless, you shall be as my mouth."
>
> Jeremiah 15:19

139

In the midst of the wilderness, God called Jeremiah to return to Him. Likewise, God calls us to return to Him, where we may receive not only healing for our hurts but a new calling and vision. The wilderness is intended to refine in us jewels of wisdom, which when set in the crown of God's calling will enable us to speak what is precious. We will become God's hands and mouth.

Questions for Reflection

1. How has God hurt you?
2. Are you holding any anger toward Him?
3. In prayer and in your journal, trust in God's grace and forgiveness. Express your deep, real feelings toward Him.

> "Come, let us return to
> the LORD; for he has
> torn, that he may heal
> us; he has stricken, and
> he will bind us up.
> After two days he will
> revive us; on the third
> day he will raise us up,
> that we may live before
> him. Let us know, let
> us press on to know
> the LORD; his going
> forth is sure as the
> dawn; he will come to
> us as the showers, as
> the spring rains that
> water the earth."
> Hosea 6:1–3

God as Our Healer

Healing is God's gracious work, but we have a part in it. We must follow the admonition of Hosea: "Come, let us return to the LORD." The call to return to God is necessary because many of us have been so broken in the wilderness that we have fled from Him. We have given up serving God and, by turning away from Him, have rejected prayer and listening to Scripture, too. We must return, but how?

Returning is an act of will, not of feeling. Out of willpower only, even if our hearts are cold and bitter, we turn to God and seek Him in prayer. Out of will, and will alone, we put one foot after another in obedience, even though we experience no joy.

Now you see the paradox. The same will that God was killing becomes, after the battle, the means by which we are restored. If we wait until feelings of warmth toward God and joy in service return, we may have to wait forever. But our wills, now set

141

on radical obedience, pull us back into the relationship where our wounded feelings cannot go.

I will explore three specific acts by which we return to God and participate in our own healing.

Beyond Willpower to Confession

First, returning to God requires confession of sin. Hatred, anger, rebellion against God—we must confess all before Him. In the wilderness we discover the depth of depravity within ourselves and our helplessness in the face of its power. We may actually have fallen deeply into sin. Confession means telling God honestly that we now know our limits. We recognize that there is no righteousness within us.

We may confess alone in the presence of God. But I have found that to really appropriate the forgiveness Jesus won for us on the cross, it is helpful to confess to God in the presence of someone else.

While in seminary, I had a heavy burden of sin from some things I had done while working in Vietnam the summer before entering seminary. I was tormented with guilt and the knowledge that I had greatly hindered the work of the Kingdom of God in that nation. Each night I went alone to the seminary chapel to pray, crying out to God to forgive me and lift the oppressive guilt.

I knew that on the cross Jesus had forgiven me. But in my heart I had no peace. Each morning after I prayed, I awoke with the same burden blotting out the sunshine. And day after day as I carried this guilt, I began to doubt my calling into ministry, and even to question my salvation.

Finally I had had enough. I sought out my best friend, Harris Ricks, who later would stand with me during my battle to accept the call to renewal ministry, and with whom I would meet Jesus. At this point he was neither minister nor priest, simply a Christian friend whom I loved and trusted. Late one evening I said to him, "Harris, let's take a walk. There are things that happened while I was in Vietnam that I must tell you about."

We walked along the wooded cross-country course at Davidson College in North Carolina as I poured out all my sin.

The only response I heard was the sound of my friend's feet plodding down the wooded path alongside me. Finally I sat down on an embankment, exhausted and ready to cry. The whole story had been told. It was a relief just to divulge my secrets.

Harris sat silently. I waited, filled with fear and embarrassment. Had I told him too much? Maybe he would laugh at me or reject me. Perhaps I had just lost my best friend.

After a long time, his voice revealing tears hidden by the darkness, he said, "Yes, you really have sinned against God. You've hindered the work of His Kingdom."

These words penetrated my soul and I began to weep.

Then he reached out and put his arm around me. "But I love you as a brother, and the good news of the Gospel is that Jesus Christ loves and forgives you."

As he said these words, a strange and wonderful thing happened. Jesus was there with us. It was He who, through my friend, had put His arm around me. I could feel the Holy Spirit, like clear, cool water flowing through me, washing away the guilt and healing the hurt. My friend had been my priest and mediator, and through him God had touched me, healed me and let me know His forgiveness.

Through this experience and many others like it, I can affirm that confession to others is one of God's gracious means of ministering to us the forgiveness that is ours through Christ's work on the cross. Jesus, who knows our weakness, commands this in Scripture: "Confess your sins to each other and pray for each other so that you may be healed. The prayer of a righteous man is powerful and effective" (James 5:16, NIV).

If you are in the wilderness—or, even better, before you are driven there, for your own spiritual growth—seek a confessor. He or she does not have to be a priest or minister, but someone with spiritual maturity who loves you and loves Christ, someone you can trust and with whom you can be totally honest.

Beyond Confession to Repentance

Returning to God in confession is not just a matter of words and tears. There must also be repentance, which implies action and change. *Repentance* in Hebrew means "to turn." Through Ezekiel God says, "Repent and turn away from your idols; and turn away your faces from all your abominations" (Ezekiel 14:6).

Imagine a person getting up from bowing down to an idol. He can confess his sin in worshiping it. He may weep and feel remorse. But as long as he still faces the statue, it is all empty words. He must get up, turn his face physically away and set his eyes and heart on Jesus. That is repentance.

As we return to God, we must concretely turn away from other things. Often for the Christian these may not be especially bad or wicked things—only what is not in God's will. How, practically speaking, do we do this? Most of what we have to turn away from is an overattachment to some idea, hope or personal relationship. What we turn toward is the invisible, intangible reality of God and walking with Him.

How do we accomplish this turning or repentance in the spiritual realm when we are living in the world? Sometimes through some physical as well as spiritual act. It helps immeasurably to recognize that decisions made in the material realm can symbolize realities in the spiritual realm. Through the Holy Spirit, who transcends and includes both heaven and earth, there is what Charles Williams called the "co-inherence" of the material and spiritual worlds.[1] At the Last Supper, for example, Jesus held out common bread and wine and said, "This is My body broken for you," and, "This is My blood poured out for you." And the co-inherence of the material and spiritual realms makes possible Jesus' promise to the Church: "I will give you the keys of the kingdom of heaven; whatever you bind on earth will be bound in heaven, and whatever you loose on earth will be loosed in heaven" (Matthew 16:19, NIV).

Anyone who has fallen in love after being attached to someone else understands that small tokens of a past affection—a hair ribbon or love letter, perhaps—must be cast away as a symbolic but actual turning toward the new object of love.

When coming out of the wilderness and walking in the new path of a surrendered will to God, I experienced many times when the Holy Spirit brought something before me and said, *Give that up*, or, *That must be thrown away*, or, *No, you can no longer do that.* In themselves these things might have seemed trivial, but I knew they symbolized deeper decisions, icebergs jutting up from the realm of the Spirit.

Here is a silly one that illustrates the point. Months before taking a team of pastors from Taiwan to visit Jesus Abbey in Korea, I had my heart set on buying a new wristwatch. I had saved my money carefully and even hoarded several gifts from Christmas for my new watch. I had saved four hundred dollars—two hundred in cash and two hundred in traveler's checks. That money was mine! In addition, I took to Korea several hundred more dollars intended for expenses and as a gift to the Abbey if there was any left over.

Our time at the Abbey was incredible. Archer Torrey and I taught that the precondition to receiving the Holy Spirit for power was surrendering our wills.

The night before the pastors were to pray to be filled with the Holy Spirit, we took an offering for the work at the Abbey. I went forward and offered all my leftover money, about one hundred fifty dollars. But as I turned away, I heard the Holy Spirit say, to my consternation, *No. Jesus needs all your cash for the work here.*

That night and all the next day, I argued with God. That other two hundred dollars was my money! It was for my watch!

But the money burned in my pocket. I knew that the real issue was not the two hundred dollars, but whether I was willing to trust and obey God for the provision to live and to do ministry.

As the day wore on and the time approached for the pastors to be filled with the Holy Spirit, I knew in my gut that there would be no expression of the power of the Spirit through me unless I surrendered my will and trusted God. The symbol of my surrendered will and radical trust was that two hundred dollars I had decreed as my own.

Just before the prayer meeting, I went up to a little chapel on the grounds and pleaded with God to let me keep the money. I know it sounds silly, but behind the issue of the money lay the frightening call to step out in a level of trust I had never before experienced. God was unrelenting in His demand: *Jesus needs all your cash for His work.* Finally I pulled it out of my pocket and flung it angrily on the altar. I was grateful that He had not demanded the traveler's checks as well!

As I left the chapel, the Holy Spirit fell on me in great power. And at the prayer meeting all the pastors were baptized in the Holy Spirit.

I learned a profound lesson from that event. To turn to God and walk with Jesus often requires some apparently trivial symbolic action that the Holy Spirit assigns you. When you obey, there are profound implications in the realm of the spirit that will affect your destiny. When you disobey, you will miss the adventure of walking with Jesus and shaping with Him a new world. For me, making that offering marked the beginning of a lifestyle of walking in faith ministry.

From my obedience in giving the two hundred dollars, I also learned that God provides all the power and provision we need to do the work of His Kingdom. Not only did He pour out the Holy Spirit on the pastors, but He gave me a new watch as well. It happened like this.

When we got to Seoul after our time at the Abbey, we all went shopping and I found just the watch I wanted. The price, to my heartbreak and disgust, was exactly four hundred dollars.

On the plane back to Taiwan, I had a long talk with God in which I thanked Him for the Korea trip and also gave up my hope of getting the watch I wanted.

The next week I happened to be walking by a jewelry store in my city. There in the window was the same model of watch I had wanted so desperately in Korea. I figured it was hopeless, but on a whim I walked in and asked the price. To my amazement I was told that it was on sale for two hundred dollars. I pulled the traveler's checks out of my wallet and bought the watch right there.

I left dancing like a little boy with a new toy. On my wrist was a new watch, but in my heart I knew it was symbolic of an even greater gift. This was the gift of faith to trust God for provision for doing His work.

Ask yourself: What is it God is asking you to repent of and to turn from? But don't stop there where it is safe. Ask the next question, too: What symbolic action is He asking you to make? Usually you have known for a long time exactly what you must do in order to be completely free to walk with Jesus out of the wilderness.

Beyond Repentance to Forgiveness

We need healing from the wilderness, and the key to receiving healing is forgiveness. Forgiveness opens the gates of our hearts so that God's grace and healing love may flow into us.

In the wilderness it is usually those closest to us, whom we love most deeply, who have hurt us most profoundly. When we love, we put away our armor, making ourselves vulnerable. We place our hearts in their hands. They are the ones who, intentionally or unintentionally, can dash our hearts to pieces. These are the people we need most to forgive.

After each of my times in the wilderness, I have had to forgive my wife, Laura. There were always things I perceived that she did to deepen my pain. Mostly, however, I have had to ask for her forgiveness. She has stood by me faithfully as I thrashed wretchedly about. She is the one who has been hurt by my wilderness times. So we have needed healing together.

Two Others We Must Forgive

Often we are angry with ourselves. We may even hate ourselves. Sometimes we must forgive ourselves just for being ourselves.

We also may need to forgive the God who made us.

Forgive God? Yes, God! He is the One ultimately responsible for our hurt and pain.

Is it not arrogant for us to think we can forgive God? Perhaps, but if so, it is the arrogance of Christians who know that in Christ they are treated not as slaves but as sons and daughters, heirs of the Kingdom, who may come boldly into the presence of God. This is no longer arrogance, but freedom of communication that issues out of the deep love God has called us to share with Him.

Whether God needs to receive our forgiveness, I do not know, but one thing is for sure: We need to give it! Our spiritual growth and physical and emotional health require it.

Are these glib words? Talking about the need to forgive is easy; doing it is nearly impossible! Isn't there something within us that clings to hurt and resentment against others (or against God) and refuses to forgive? As long as we refuse to forgive, we still have power over the one who injured us. In a sick sort of way we hold them in our debt. For some, for whom the wound is very deep, to give up that power over the other is impossible. But we must overcome all obstacles and forgive; otherwise our hearts will remain broken. Our refusal to forgive will bury the hurt deep within us where, like an insidious cancer, it will grow, killing all joy and life and blocking the inflow of God's healing Spirit.

Unforgiveness does indeed give us power over the other, but even more, it is a force that holds us in bondage. Jesus bluntly told us the end of unforgiveness: "If you forgive men when they sin against you, your heavenly Father will also forgive you. But if you do not forgive men their sins, your Father will not forgive your sins" (Matthew 6:14–15, NIV).

What if we cannot forgive God? That is the way of eternal death.

Forgiving God for How He Made Me

I have had to forgive God after each of my times in the wilderness. Often I had to forgive Him for what sent me into the wilderness to begin with. Once it was for making me the way I am.

One of my biggest struggles in life was that I was born with dyslexia or learning disabilities. I could not read until I was past third grade, which I failed. My spelling is a disaster and my writing illegible even to myself. Growing up with this disability left layer after layer of hurt and rejection.

In grade school, Friday was hell day for me. That was the day of our spelling test, which week after week I failed. Worse, it was the day of the spelling bee. The students always chose teams and neither team ever wanted me. When the teacher had to assign me to one of the teams, they all hooted and booed. "Not him!" they shouted. "We'll lose!" I laughed and hooted back, but cried after class in the boys' room.

All through school I struggled with this disability. My parents were concerned when my brothers and sisters came home with anything less then A's, but they celebrated if I managed C's. It was only by brutal hard work and not a few miracles that I made it through Davidson College and into the Doctor of Ministry Program at Union Seminary. But I had a deep fear that because I could not write or spell, God could never use me and I would be useless in His Kingdom. Adding to my hopelessness, I knew deep down that, even though I was called to the mission field, I had failed Spanish, Latin, Hebrew and German and had made D's in English. It would be impossible, I concluded, ever to learn a foreign language.

All this left me with a lot of anger and insecurity. But my deepest resentment was against God, who had cursed me with a restless calling and at the same time created me with learning disabilities.

I would have been completely bound up with this hurt had it not been for a retreat over Pentecost that Laura and I attended while short-term missionaries in Korea. This weekend changed my life profoundly.

On the last night Laura received a leading from the Holy Spirit that God was going to do something about my dyslexia. She gathered a large group of missionaries, both Protestant and Catholic, to pray for me.

As they laid hands on me, the Lord brought back vivid images of the spelling bees, my jeering classmates and the faces of my teachers. I was told to forgive them. And I did. I was able to forgive myself, too. Finally it was God before me.

I knew He was there in the prayer circle with me through the love of all the people who had gathered around. I felt Him saying to me, *I have given you your dyslexia as a gift. Receive it, and receive me!*

With this I felt all my anger being washed away. I sensed the images of my jeering classmates losing their power over me. And I was able to forgive God.

As I did, I was caught up in a vision of how He was calling and empowering me to work for His glory.

I was not healed of my dyslexia that night. Rather I was healed of the hurt within my heart and enabled to forgive God. I still cannot spell or write! But I know I am called anyway, and that God will use me in spite of, or perhaps because of, my disability.[2] And as I look back in amazement, I see that He has.

How about You?

Return to your own situation. Undoubtedly some people have hurt you. Perhaps their faces dance before your mind's eye each time you try to pray. There is only one way out of your wilderness, and that is to forgive them—all of them, including God.

This forgiveness is the most difficult of all. But think of Jesus hanging in agony on the cross, His life's blood flowing away. He was looking down at His own people, whom He loved and had come to save. But they had misunderstood and finally rejected Him. Abandoned by God, rejected by His own people,

150

Jesus must have been filled with despair. In the Apostles' Creed we say that Jesus "descended into hell." Surely part of that descent was this abandonment. Yet Jesus said, "Father, forgive them; for they know not what they do" (Luke 23:34).

Pray that God will let you return to Him. Pray that He will give you, as He did Jesus on the cross, the grace to forgive even Him.

Questions for Reflection

1. Of what specifically is the Holy Spirit calling you to repent?
2. There is real power in confessing our sins to one another, as we are urged to do in James 5:16: "Therefore confess your sins to each other and pray for each other so that you may be healed" (NIV). Find someone to whom you may confess.
3. What actions are you called to take that you discern to be symbolic of deeper decisions in the realm of the Spirit?

Part *five*

Out of the
Wilderness

Then a voice said to him, "What are you doing here, Elijah?" He replied, "I have been very zealous for the LORD God Almighty. The Israelites have rejected your covenant, broken down your altars, and put your prophets to death with the sword. I am the only one left, and now they are trying to kill me too." The LORD said to him, "Go back the way you came, and go to the Desert of Damascus. When you get there, anoint Hazael king over Aram."
1 Kings 19:12–15, NIV

Called into God's Service

We now approach the conclusion of the long and often dismal journey through the wilderness. Why did God put us through this hell? Sometimes we find no clear answer until we see Jesus face to face and "I know even as also I am known" (1 Corinthians 13:12, KJV). Sometimes we make sense of the course of our lives, especially the meaninglessness and pain of the wilderness, only from the vantage point of the passing years. From that distance we may be astonished to find the wilderness times shining like golden threads in the plain-woven tapestry of our lives.

While I was in the wilderness, I hated it and could see none of its purpose. Today, having been healed from the hurt and given distance by the passing of time, I relish wilderness experiences as God's outrageous, undeserved gifts to me. They were times of extraordinary depth of engagement with Him that resulted in life, wisdom and calling.

In this final section we will discuss four ingredients for walking out of wilderness into usefulness to God's Kingdom: hearing God's calling; receiving His empowerment to carry out that calling; nurturing intimacy with Jesus; and developing the ability to face the emptiness.

Wilderness reduces us to silence and causes us to despair of ourselves. When we reach this point, usually after much longer than we thought we could endure, God calls us into His service. He may confirm and deepen a present calling or He may give new calling.

God May Affirm and Deepen Our Present Calling

After a time of extraordinary service to God, Elijah was driven into the wilderness by God's silence. When God spoke at last, it was almost a rebuke: "Elijah! What are you doing here?" The wilderness was not the place of Elijah's work as a prophet. But once he knew he had God's ear, he stated his complaint about his field of service. God's plan was a failure, he said. The covenant was broken, the other prophets had been killed and the king was trying to kill him, too.

God's only answer was simple and terrible: to call Elijah back to the hard work of being a prophet of judgment. "Go back the way you came," God told him (1 Kings 19:15, NIV). Elijah's mission was to complete the work he had begun and to set the next phase in motion by anointing Elisha to follow him as prophet.

So it may be with us. After the wilderness we are sent right back to where we came from to complete the work we have been given. Having been through the wilderness, we may find our circumstances the same, but we are not the same. Transformation worked in us during wilderness times enables God to use us more freely and deeply to accomplish our calling.

You can usually tell when people have been through the wilderness. They bear the marks of suffering. There is a depth to them, a wisdom, a love that is not their own. They speak about God and the things of God out of the book of their own lived experience, as if they really know Jesus Christ and the devil. The fire of meeting both has seared their souls. Above all, people who have been through the wilderness are transparent to the presence, suffering, love and power of the Holy Spirit. There is the sparkle of the Kingdom of God about them, and they experience the Kingdom—wherever they are and whatever their calling—as real.

Accepting Our Calling and Putting Down Roots

Over my mother-in-law's kitchen sink is a sign inscribed *Bloom Where You're Planted.* I used to hate that sign! In the wilderness I did not want to stay where I was planted. I wanted a new call, a new context—anywhere other than where I was.

While in the wilderness we may have fought against our calling or resented our state such as marriage or singleness. We may have chafed at our limitations and envied the gifts expressed by others. But after the wilderness, in which we died to ourselves, we find a deep peacefulness about the place to which we are called and a calm acceptance of our true gifts and potential.

Peaceful resignation to our place and calling is a particular fruit of the wilderness of midlife crisis. It certainly was for me. I have already described the crisis that descended on me like an avalanche and my soul-deep restlessness about everything in my life. About four years later, after walking in faithfulness to Jesus Christ out of raw obedience, I woke up one day and found the restlessness gone. Just gone! I looked at my wife, whom I love with all my heart, and at my wonderful children, and at my work, and wondered how I could ever have been dissatisfied. Considering my gifts and calling, which I had despised, I said, "Why, yes, Lord! You in Your wisdom have placed me in a context and calling that fit my gifts and who I am. And, yes, though I am not a John Calvin or an Einstein, and I still can't spell, and You know all my other weaknesses, I'm just me, and that's just fine."

When we come to this place of acceptance, we can truly bloom where we are planted. And only when we finally let ourselves be planted can we start to bloom by recognizing the moments of opportunity the Holy Spirit will bring us.

Bringing into Balance the Inward and Outward Work of the Holy Spirit

The process of trudging through the wilderness, with its temptations and wrestling with God, is meant to deepen our relationship with God, and thus our usefulness in His Kingdom. Many people, after receiving the Holy Spirit, are led into the wilderness as a form of spiritual boot camp, to learn how to minister in the power of the Holy Spirit. Without this wilderness training, which compels us to grow in holiness, we all too easily misuse the gifts.

In the Bible we generally find that only those who endured great suffering—like Joseph, Moses, Elijah, Peter and Paul— were trusted with great power. Without the wilderness experience, no matter how true our doctrine, we are prone to the arrogant assumption that the gifts and power are our own. An even deeper deception is that *we* are our own!

John Calvin, reflecting on 1 Corinthians 6:19, lay before us our condition and the basis of our calling into service:

> We are not our own: let not our reason nor our wills, therefore, sway our plans and deeds. We are not our own: let us therefore not set it as our goal to seek what is expedient for us according to the flesh. We are not our own: insofar as we can, let us therefore forget ourselves and all that is ours. Conversely, we are God's. Let us, therefore, live for Him and die for Him. We are God's. Let His wisdom and will rule all our actions. We are God's: let all the parts of our life accordingly strive toward Him as our only lawful goal.[1]

It is to teach us that we are not our own that God may have driven us into the wilderness. Only as we recognize that we are not our own are we free to obey God's Word and give ourselves over to His purpose and calling. When this fact of our condition has been seared into our hearts, God can trust us with the gifts and power of the Holy Spirit. Only then can we share in the great work of building the Kingdom of God with Him for His everlasting glory.

Deepening the Call to Healing Ministry

After I experienced a baptism in the Holy Spirit, I was anointed and called into a ministry of healing, especially inner healing. It was exciting to watch God work through me to heal and restore others! I also enjoyed the compliments and affirmations I received after the Spirit had worked.

Soon afterward, however, I was driven into a time of wilderness. One night I prayed in despair, "God, why again? I thought I was finished with the wilderness. Why the temptations and struggles again? Why the pain?"

Within my own thoughts, I heard the Holy Spirit whisper the following words:

I have called you to be a healer.
But before My servants can heal, they must first be broken.
It is for you to live with a broken heart,
With a scar within the depths of your soul
marking you forever as a sinner,
as one who has no right to stand in My presence.
But awareness of your weakness, and that you are marked,
will be the source of your strength . . .
for now you know your utter weakness.

With these words spoken to my heart, I realized I had taken the gift of healing as my own. As obviously wrong as it looks on paper, my ego wanted to take possession of this gift and use it for my glory. The wilderness taught me that our treasure is contained in earthen vessels—broken vessels at that! Brokenness is also important for the nature of the gift. Only as I knew my own wounded heart would I be able to feel the pain of others and be the means, the wounded healer, that Jesus would use to heal them.

The wilderness did not change my calling into healing ministry; it deepened it. It also made it safe for me to receive the gifts and power to fulfill the ministry. For then I knew with my whole being that the source of blessing was God and God alone.

Where are you? Are you walking out of the wilderness? Are you finding a new peace about where you are? If so, settle down and, for a season, enjoy your place. Expect God to begin to open your eyes to possibilities for love, service and action that, in your restlessness to leave, you could not see. Now, with roots in the soil of a particular place, you can start to grow and bloom. Anticipate new empowerment and effectiveness.

Maybe, on the other hand, you are still restless and your soul is disturbed by the rumblings of new vision and calling. If so, consider the possibility that God's purpose for sending you into the wilderness is to drive you from your present contentment and into the risk of hearing His new calling, to be blown away by a new vision. You may look forward to a major relocation— not just geographic, but in the realm of the Spirit.

God May Give Us a New Calling

Besides deepening our present call, the wilderness may prepare us for a radically new calling and empowerment. This was Moses' case. While a prince in Egypt, he was seized by indignation about the oppression of his people by the Egyptians. Driven by anger to right the wrong, he murdered an Egyptian taskmaster.

Such concern for justice is noble, but there was too much of Moses and not enough of God. So the adopted son of Pharaoh's daughter was sent into the wilderness—the literal wilderness— for forty long years. There the Moses of Egypt died, along with his dreams, ambitions and, most likely, his royal ego. They had to die in order to make room for God's plans that were so outrageous, so impossible and so vast that only a man who had died to himself could receive them.

More than by plans, Moses was being prepared to be overshadowed, like the virgin Mary, by God Himself. He was to be consumed by God. Our calling to new work, after all, is never really to a work or project but to a new level of intimacy with God.

When the wilderness had done its job, God met Moses in the burning bush:

> "The cry of the Israelites has reached me, and I have seen the way the Egyptians are oppressing them. So now, go. I am sending you to Pharaoh to bring my people the Israelites out of Egypt."
>
> Exodus 3:9–10, NIV

God, the Creator of the universe, was right there before this now thoroughly humbled shepherd. He gave His name, as never before, to humanity: "I AM WHO I AM" (Exodus 3:14). And out of this meeting Moses was given the mission not only to bring God's people out of slavery, but to form them into a nation. Without God this was a mission utterly impossible. Moses himself, without being filled with God, would never have conceived anything so audacious.

Meeting Jesus in Deeper Intimacy

After we, too, have been silenced and reduced to helplessness, God wants to meet us and blow our minds with a vision of Himself, His Kingdom and our part in it. The calling of the Christian always grows out of a meeting with Jesus Christ. We are not given a program or project. Rather, we are given a relationship with the Christ, who says to us, "Come, follow Me." The ultimate purpose of the wilderness: to prepare us for a new level of intimacy with Jesus.

During the times I have spent in the wilderness, Oswald Chambers' devotional *My Utmost for His Highest* has spoken

161

to my heart and helped prepare me for meeting with Jesus Christ. Chambers was writing about Paul's Damascus road experience:

> Paul was not given a message or a doctrine to proclaim; he was brought into a vivid, personal, overmastering relationship to Jesus Christ. Verse 16 [of Acts 26] is immensely command-ing—"to make thee a minister and a witness." There is nothing there apart from the personal relationship. Paul was devoted to a Person not to a cause. He was absolutely Jesus Christ's, he saw nothing else, he lived for nothing else.[2]

As I sought purpose and direction, these words pulled me like gravity away from seeking plans or grandiose projects, as I am prone to do, and to pray for and expect a visitation from Jesus Christ Himself.

On the edges of the wilderness, an encounter with Jesus may come in a variety of ways. It may take place in a trackless waste or a burning bush of mystical experience. The Holy Spirit may make vivid and alive His Word in your heart. Or a new depth of intimacy with Jesus may come through the fellowship and warm embrace of His Body, your brothers and sisters. The Holy Spirit is immensely creative, so you cannot predict how the meeting will come to you. Just know that Jesus' gracious pur-pose of sending you into the hell of the wilderness is to prepare you for such an encounter.

Jesus, the Lover of your soul, yearns for this opportunity to bring you to Himself and to give you the work for which you were created. "We are God's workmanship, created in Christ Jesus to do good works, which God prepared in advance for us to do" (Ephesians 2:10, NIV). The only way you can know who you really are and what you are called to do is to meet Jesus.

Receiving New Vision for Ministry

In my life it has been at the end of the wilderness that I have met Jesus, and each of these meetings has resulted in new vision and calling. One such meeting took place over a six-month period while I prayed for vision for Presbyterian and Reformed Renewal Ministries International. This was after the battle of opposing wills that I described in an earlier chapter.

When I accepted the call to be the executive director of PRRMI, I landed in an organization that was itself in the depths of wilderness, so we were a good match. The charismatic wave of the Holy Spirit, which in the 1960s had gotten the PRRMI boat afloat, had by the 1990s ebbed away. PRRMI was left beached, with no popular movement to carry the organization. Most of the original leaders had moved powerfully in the anointing of the Holy Spirit but had not prepared leaders to succeed them. They had been Elijahs who had called few Elishas. Many had now retired. Some had died. Brick Bradford, the founding general secretary, had worked heroically to keep the ministry on track with the work of the Holy Spirit, but it was like swimming against the current.

When I came to PRRMI I had no plans, only the vision I had been given in the mystical encounter on the mountain in Korea—for an international ministry of renewal for the worldwide advancement of God's Kingdom. This was all I had. Both PRRMI and I had come through the wilderness. We had no illusions of having anything in our own strength. We were both emptyhanded and desperate.

Usually it is only after a church or organization has been through the wilderness that it becomes malleable and may be shaped by new vision and calling. That is where PRRMI was. That part was exciting. The terrifying part was that it had little by way of financial, spiritual or organizational support.

This state of affairs was summed up well for me the first time I had lunch in a cafeteria in Oklahoma City with the general secretary and the president of the board. As I reached for a nice piece of fish, Brick said jokingly, "No! Remember, you're about to take over an organization that's nearly bankrupt!" So I selected a small salad instead—with not a few qualms about the task that lay ahead.

When I returned to North Carolina to report all this to Laura, we wondered if we had made a mistake in accepting the call. Once again, recognizing my utter helplessness drove me up to a mountain in prayer. I wrestled with God beside the same stream in Montreat where, with Harris at my side, I had died to my own will and accepted the call to this organization.

That night had been my Gethsemane. This battle was different. It was not a conflict of opposing wills, since my will was set on obedience. No, now my role was as intercessor calling down God's vision for His own work.

"Lord," I prayed, "now that You've gotten me here, what is it You want me to do? How is it that PRRMI is to share in the worldwide movement of Your Holy Spirit?"

Over the weeks, often sitting beside the same stream, I became aware again and again of Someone with me. Jesus embraced me with His presence. He spoke to me through the Bible and through others. I enjoyed no dramatic mystical encounters, as I had on the mountain in Korea. But gradually, piece by piece, a vision came together that fired my heart and directed my thoughts. As I invited the PRRMI board of directors to join me in this process, it was like staring at the scattered pieces of a jigsaw puzzle and beginning to see where first one piece, and then another, fit.

Finally all the pieces came together. I knew in my heart that the vision and marching orders, for me and for the organization, were this: "Exalting Jesus Christ and igniting the Church in the power of the Holy Spirit, through prayer, leadership development, congregational renewal and mission outreach, so that the Church may be empowered to do all that Christ commands."

This vision, as I have obeyed the leading of the Holy Spirit and stepped out in risk-taking faith, has birthed program ministry and organization. It has become the means of fulfilling the original calling that I received in Korea of international renewal ministry to advance God's Kingdom.

What About You?

Where are you in your wilderness journey? Has Jesus met you yet? Has He given you a calling and vision for the work that lies ahead? If in your battles with God you have surrendered your will but have not yet been called, do not rest! Go up the mountain and, in prayer, seek God until He tells you what your calling is. Remind Him of your sufferings in the wilderness, and that the task of following Jesus was not your idea but His. Tell Him urgently that you want to follow but cannot unless He speaks to you and gives you a clear call and vision. Stay in this mode of prayer until you know what you are to do.

Above all, lift to Him the emptiness in your soul, and the restless yearning for relationship and meaning that He placed there when He created you and stamped you with His image. Seek God until He meets you at your own burning bush. Then walk in obedience and trust Him.

Now let's examine the second fruit of the wilderness: the empowerment to accomplish God's call.

Questions for Reflection

1. Is God calling you to "bloom where you're planted" through the wilderness experience? Is He calling you to greater usefulness and commitment in the place where you are?
2. Does the restlessness persist? Is He calling you to new direction, new location, new ministry?
3. Write your personal vision of what you believe God is calling you to become and to do.

He told them, "This is what is written: The Christ will suffer and rise from the dead on the third day, and repentance and forgiveness of sins will be preached in his name to all nations, beginning at Jerusalem. You are witnesses of these things. I am going to send you what my Father has promised; but stay in the city until you have been clothed with power from on high."

Luke 24:46–49, NIV

Out of the Wilderness into New Empowerment

Being driven into the wilderness may, as in the case of Jesus, follow the Holy Spirit's falling upon us. At other times the process is reversed: We are driven by the wilderness so completely to despair of ourselves that we are ready to welcome Jesus to baptize us with the Holy Spirit.[1] As the wilderness prepares us to receive a new or deeper calling, so, too, it prepares us to receive the Holy Spirit's power to fulfill this calling.

In the New Testament, God's humanly impossible calling and commission are always packaged with the promise of the means to accomplish it. After the resurrection Jesus commissioned His disciples with these words: "You are witnesses of these things" (Luke 24:48). Then He promised that they would be "clothed with power from on high" (verse 49) as the means to fulfill this extraordinary commission.

Peter, a man greatly empowered by the Holy Spirit, was able to receive this power because he had been broken. But before

166

his wilderness of denying Jesus and being sifted by Satan, Peter had experienced the Holy Spirit falling on him for power. Luke records the beginning of the power ministry of Peter and the other disciples:

> When Jesus had called the Twelve together, he gave them power and authority to drive out all demons and to cure diseases, and he sent them out to preach the kingdom of God and to heal the sick.
>
> Luke 9:1–2, NIV

How was this possible? Was this not before Pentecost? According to John 7:39, "The Spirit had not been given, because Jesus was not yet glorified." This is not the place to explain the workings of the Holy Spirit; I have tried to do that elsewhere. The important thing to know is that the disciples, in this first commissioning, were given the power of the Holy Spirit because the Spirit fell on them in the way He fell on the Old Testament prophets, priests and kings. The Spirit was upon these disciples as He had fallen upon Isaiah, Samson, Balaam and even Balaam's ass!

So before Pentecost Peter had tasted the power of the Holy Spirit—as an Old Testament man. He was bold and effective in ministry, and most likely he joined with the 72 in rejoicing, "Lord, even the demons submit to us in your name" (Luke 10:17, NIV).

God worked greatly through Peter and the rest, but they were not yet ready to be trusted with the full expression of the Holy Spirit's gifts and power. As with Moses in Egypt, there was too much of Peter in Peter to entrust him with either God's power or His vision. So God sent Peter into the wilderness, where he went through the fire of being tested by Satan. Peter died with the crow of the rooster; his ego and self-confidence were shattered.

On the beach after the resurrection, with Jesus' command for Peter to "feed my sheep" (John 21:17), the Lord restored Peter's calling but not his anointing. That was to wait until the Day of Pentecost.

167

At Pentecost the Holy Spirit again came upon Peter (as well as on the other disciples), granting great power and supernatural gifts for the accomplishment of Jesus' work. Now the power rested on a man who had died to self and was alive in Jesus—a man clearly called and on fire with Jesus' mission and vision.

Discovering What We Need for Ministry

While Laura and I were students at seminary, I was taught to be proud of my gifts and capacities. I did not think I really needed God to do ministry. I planned to serve God in the Church, of course. But the concept of God speaking, preaching and ministering through someone was alien to me. Further, I had no idea practically how this would be done. At seminary I learned that the way to serve God effectively was to become an expert preacher—good with words, perceptive in Bible study and well organized in presentation. Pastoral care was a matter of showing compassion and knowing the right proven techniques.

The bottom line: I was arrogant and self-sufficient.

God changed this human-powered, me-centered approach by sending my wife and me to Korea for a year during our third year of seminary to do teaching and preaching. As newly married short-term missionaries, we landed not only in a foreign country but in a short but intense wilderness. Laura went through severe culture shock, while I found my seminary training and carefully honed pastoral skills useless. Being clever with words in the pulpit is ineffectual when your hearers do not speak your language and you can barely speak theirs! Further, the nice pastoral care approaches from seminary were powerless in dealing with demons.

During this wilderness testing time, I received one lesson after another in my own helplessness and in the fact that a seminary education does not automatically open doors for effective ministry. Despite my best efforts I was finding myself useless.

Brutally God taught Laura and me what seminary had failed to teach us: It is not we who do ministry, but the Holy Spirit who does it through us. We made this discovery as we confronted our own helplessness and as we spent time with other missionaries through whom the Holy Spirit was working in great power.

Once at a Korean dinner, our host, a Presbyterian evangelist, fell asleep at the table between courses. When we woke him up with a plate of hot *kimchee,* he confessed that he had preached seventeen different sermons that week, and it was only Friday.

"Seventeen sermons!" I exclaimed. "How do you do it? It's all I can do to preach once a week."

"Oh, I don't do it," he replied. "The Holy Spirit does it. I just have to get myself there, and that's exhausting. The preaching is the easy part, because it's not me."

I just looked at him in amazement.

Later he and his wife told Laura and me that they had been not only useless in ministry in Korea, but were at the stage of burnout. They had tried very hard to follow Jesus and had striven to be model missionaries, but it was not working. They were exhausted, their marriage was in trouble, their health was in danger from overwork and poor diet and they were ready to quit the mission field. At this point, in deep wilderness and desperate, they came across a book on the Holy Spirit. Later they prayed to be filled with the Spirit. That was when they stopped doing the ministry in their own strength and God began to do it through them.

Hearing reports like this and seeing the undeniable fruit of changed lives drove Laura and me to explore the empowering, gift-giving work of the Holy Spirit. We had many theological questions and a Western worldview that denied the possibility of God working and speaking today. We had our own self-sufficiency and major prejudice against Pentecostal and charismatic experience. Finally, however, the wilderness drove us to such desperation that we cried out to God to be filled with the Holy Spirit. Without it we knew we were useless in service to Jesus Christ.

I will tell my part of this story later, but I have asked Laura to tell hers first, to demonstrate the diversity of the experience.

Laura's Experience: Surprised by the Holy Spirit

My year in Korea was extremely difficult. Since Brad had lived there while attending high school, he knew many people, spoke some Korean and was simply going home. For me, however, it was like landing in an alien culture. Our living situation at the theological seminary where we taught was difficult. During the winter we were cold and had no running water or plumbing for four frozen months. The market was located a mile walk down the mountain. And Seoul, where English-speaking friends lived, was an hour away by bus.

As a woman in a chauvinistic culture, I was often treated as a nonperson. It was hard to get used to not being looked at or spoken to. Brad received compliments on what a wonderful wife he had because I was quiet. I had little choice, of course, not being able to speak the language! But this treatment hurt my pride and I responded by being more culturally arrogant.

While in America I had been turned off by the charismatic renewal. Occasionally we had attended prayer and praise meetings out of curiosity and amusement. But in Korea, driven by great spiritual need as well as by the desire for English-speaking friends, we spent a lot of time in the homes of several Presbyterian missionaries. They had a vibrant faith and were matter-of-fact about the role of the Holy Spirit in their successful mission work.

Months later I reached a low point. Sick of the culture and the difficulties of daily living, I questioned whether I could ever be an effective minister. Lonely and beaten down, I wondered how I could keep going.

About this time Brad and I attended a monthly prayer meeting with Protestant and Catholic missionaries from all over Korea. One evening I was sitting in the circle listening to the singing and praying, sensing the warmth and support of the group. Then I noticed that my tongue was moving. I just let it go; it felt comfortable and good. I didn't think anyone noticed anything happening to me, nor did I tell anyone.

The next morning I awoke with the most wonderful sense that God had given me a gift. It was as if there were some precious jewel buried within me. I felt like a child waking up early on Christmas Day with a sense of wonder and excitement.

This marked a turning point for me. For the first time I found the courage to share my faith with others. Life in the Holy Spirit became real and I began, to my great delight, to grow in the Spirit's gifts.[2]

Brad's Experience: Blown Away by the Spirit's Power

My own encounter with the Holy Spirit happened while Laura and I were visiting Jesus Abbey in the mountains of South Korea. Just after the community finished supper and before the worship service started, I asked Archer Torrey, director of the Abbey, to pray for me. I wanted prayer before the service because I was afraid the music would provide the occasion for psychological manipulation; and if anything was to happen, I wanted it to be real! I was especially afraid I would speak in tongues, and the last thing I wanted was to look like some kind of fool.

Archer and other members of the community gathered around me, laying on hands. Archer prayed a disappointingly simple prayer: "Lord, we give You thanks that You have used Brad in the past. Now please baptize him with Your Holy Spirit, that he may be even more useful to You in the future. And, by the way, Lord, please give him the gift of tongues."

Now why did he have to go and mess everything up by throwing in that second part? I thought. Then I began to wonder, *Was that all? Nothing's going to happen!*

The next moment I was overwhelmed with a sense of the presence of God. Jesus was right there beside me pouring buckets of love over me. It was so delicious and wonderful that I found myself laughing aloud for joy. In between the laughter I was speaking in a language I had not learned that was bursting spontaneously from my lips. In the midst of all this power, which

171

seemed to be flowing over me like a waterfall, I felt Jesus calling me to follow Him into ministry for His glory. It was absolutely glorious! I spent the rest of the night in the chapel in prayer.

The very next morning, through a communication breakdown with my wife, the Lord let me know without a doubt that my entire sanctification was a long way off!

Right after this experience, however, several visible effects made me know that something profound had indeed taken place. For Laura and me, a profound shift took place in our lives and ministry. God started to bestow the gifts of the Holy Spirit to do the ministry through us. We continued to work hard, of course, preparing for teaching and preaching, keeping in mind biblical theology, striving to understand the dynamics of pastoral care. But we experienced power! Things actually started to happen when we prayed, preached or ministered. As a regular part of our Christian lives, we started to experience the Holy Spirit falling upon us or filling us, enabling us to do God's work.

This was immensely exciting. Whole new vistas opened up. The experience of being baptized in the Holy Spirit blew my mind. I figured I had arrived in the Promised Land.

I could not have been more mistaken. What followed, as I have already reported, was being driven into the worst wilderness of my life during my time of parish ministry. For me, empowerment preceded wilderness. But the door had been opened to the new dimension of the Holy Spirit's gifts and power, and that made all the difference in surviving the wilderness experiences I describe in this book.

Have You Received the Power Yet?

Preparing to receive the infilling of the Holy Spirit is one of the most important fruits of the wilderness. If you read the lives of great servants of God like Dwight L. Moody, St. Theresa of Avila, John Calvin, John Bunyan and St. Ignatius, you will see that they all went through a wilderness that drove them to help-lessness. After encounters with the living God, however, they moved in His power to fulfill His vision. Moody and others called this encounter with God "the baptism with the Holy Spirit." Others referred to "being filled with the Holy Spirit." Still others reported having been met by God in majesty and glory.

Where are you in your ministry and life? Are you bearing good fruit that gives glory to Jesus Christ? Are you shaping reality around you to reflect the Kingdom of God? Is God doing His work through you, or are you striving in your own strength to do His work? Have you been given a call from God that staggers you with its human impossibility? If you are finding yourself helpless, that is good! You are right where the Holy Spirit wants you.

Don't get hung up on terms like *baptism with the Holy Spirit, being filled with the Holy Spirit* or *the Spirit upon.* Rather, let your desperate wilderness situation drive you to seek and receive Jesus' promised preparation for ministry: the gift of the Holy Spirit.

Questions for Reflection

1. Have you found yourself powerless to do Christ's work effectively, while there is burning within you a love for Jesus and a clear calling to follow Him?
2. Explore the biblical promises about the empowering work of the Holy Spirit.
3. In prayer ask Jesus to fill you with the Holy Spirit for the gifts, power and guidance you need to do His work.

18

When the devil had
finished all this temp-
ting, he left him until
an opportune time.
Jesus returned to Gali-
lee in the power of the
Spirit, and news about
him spread through
the whole countryside.
Luke 4:13–14, NIV

Beyond Wilderness

Walking with Jesus in Intimacy and Fruitfulness

We now come to the end of the wilderness journey. It is not an end at all, but the beginning of new fruitfulness in the Kingdom of God.

Jesus returned to Galilee after the wilderness temptation "in the power of the Spirit" (Luke 4:14, NIV). There was a force-fulness and immediacy about His work. He preached the Kingdom of God with power. The sick were healed, demons were cast out and crowds were fed miraculously. Jesus silenced the wind and waves and walked on the water. He wept broken-hearted at the tomb of Lazarus and groaned with compassion for others' suffering. In the Transfiguration, and as Jesus sought regular refuge in the lonely places for prayer, we catch glimpses of a depth of intimacy with His Father far surpassing that of Moses, who talked to God face to face. In the midst of all this,

174

Jesus moved with singleminded purpose toward Jerusalem for the completion of His earthly mission.

All this fruit—the intimacy, the power, the obedience—was nurtured in the wilderness.

In these final chapters we have been discussing the ingredients for walking out of wilderness into usefulness to God's Kingdom. We have looked at calling and empowerment. Now we conclude with two other fruits of the wilderness essential for walking with Jesus in effective ministry: intimacy with Him and the ability to face the emptiness. One touches the inward connection of our hearts to Jesus' heart, and the other is an inward attitude that provides the space for Jesus to act in and through us.

Growing in Intimacy with Jesus Christ

Jesus said, "I am the vine; you are the branches. If a man remains in me and I in him, he will bear much fruit; apart from me you can do nothing" (John 15:5, NIV). In these words Jesus made it clear that the only basis for fruitfulness in the Kingdom of God is intimacy with Him. It is the same basis that Jesus Himself had for fruitfulness in ministry. "The Son can do nothing of his own accord," He said, "but only what he sees the Father doing" (John 5:19). When we are born again, we are welcomed into the same intimate relationship that Jesus had with His *Abba* (see Romans 8:15).

There is little to add, for the whole point of wilderness and of this book has been to coax, drive or woo us to this intimacy with Jesus Christ. Indeed, the sole reason Jesus allows us to be driven into the wilderness is to bring us to Himself. In chapter 16 we discussed intimacy with Jesus as the basis for experiencing a call. In chapter 17 it is the basis for empowerment. In this final chapter I conclude that the great gift of the wilderness, through which we discover and maintain this intimacy, is prayer.

God's intention for sending us into the wilderness is to make us people of prayer like Moses and Jesus. Prayer lies at the heart of our relationship with God. If we have not become people of prayer, we have not yet learned the wilderness lesson and are due to be sent back. Pray to be sent back! If, on the other hand, God and Satan have done their best and you have not become a person of prayer, but are still alive to your own will and insist on living life your own way, God may decide to toss you on the scrap heap of His saved but useless servants.

Discovering Prayer

As the wilderness drove me deeper toward God, I was terrified of getting too close. I did not want to pray. At the same time, as layer after layer of self-sufficiency was torn away, I was drawn with an insatiable desire for Him. In the dryness of the wilderness, the cry of the psalmist became my cry: "O God, you are my God, earnestly I seek you; my soul thirsts for you, my body longs for you, in a dry and weary land where there is no water" (Psalm 63:1, NIV). Through this terrible, soul-deep dryness, God drew me into intimacy with Himself.

Yet I was terrified because I knew what He wanted—all of me! He, with fiery, all-consuming love, wanted not only my radical, wholehearted obedience, but my radical, no-holds-barred, singleminded love. The wilderness work was bringing me into the orb of God's love and to the despairing recognition that such love and obedience were humanly impossible. The end of the journey, and the beginning of intimacy, was letting go and letting God do in me what was impossible for me to do on my own. This is the process of dying to ourselves, of letting God kill us.

While this was taking place, I was sure it was the very end of me. It was like walking through a door appearing to open out into utter emptiness—only to find, once I walked through it, that there was instead of nothingness a firm and surprising reality.

One of the biggest surprises was what happened to my prayer life. Praying became a happy necessity, like breathing. It was completely, supernaturally natural! Prayer became a gift given by the Holy Spirit, who prayed through me and caught me up in the loop of love, communion and communication among Father, Son and Holy Spirit. The life of prayer, I found, was no longer a solitary walk with God, but living and breathing in fellowship with the Holy Spirit and with others, in whom I discovered supernatural intimacy. We are all part of the fellowship of the Spirit of Jesus who will love and live forever.

The fellowship of prayer transcends nations and race, time and space. It embraces both the living and the dead—all who are alive in Jesus.

Being Driven up the Mountain

I discovered another aspect of prayer that may also happen to you. The Holy Spirit invited me regularly back into aloneness with God, as He did again and again with Jesus. These times up the mountain with God in prayer are mini-wildernesses. They are places of communion and sometimes of testing; places of listening to God and of getting direction for how to walk with Jesus during the times when daily life muddies our vision and distorts our view.

Going up the mountain is dying to oneself every day. But if we practice this, we may be spared the trauma of being sent back into some big wilderness to get killed all over again. Go up the mountain! Don't get discouraged and give up on enjoying this mountaintop fellowship if you live on the coast or on the flatlands with no mountains in sight. To go up the mountain is a journey of the spirit. It is to flee with Jesus to the lonely places of the heart when you put aside all else to be with God in prayer. You can do this anywhere.

If we are to continue to grow in intimacy with Jesus Christ, solitary times on the mountain must happen wherever we are and to all of us called to usefulness to God.

Facing Emptiness: Making Space for Jesus to Work

If the purpose of wilderness is to get us to the point where it is not we working, but Jesus working in and through us, have you ever pondered the question as to how, practically speaking, this happens?

You may have read the wonderful novel called *In His Steps* by Charles Sheldon. It describes the life-transforming adventures that take place when a pastor and congregation start to ask, "In this situation, what would Jesus do?" Then they do what they believe Jesus would have done.

This classic has called millions to action and obedience. But I am interested in another question: If we believe Jesus is alive today and working through His Spirit, how does He do His work? That question is not "What would Jesus do?" but, "What is Jesus actually doing?" (And there is another novel to be written on that inquiry!)

Here I want to identify one of the strangest fruits of the wilderness—the gift to face the emptiness, which is the first step in cooperating with Jesus in power ministry.

In the book of Revelation we find this intriguing verse:

> When the Lamb opened the seventh seal, there was silence in heaven for about half an hour. Then I saw the seven angels who stand before God, and seven trumpets were given to them.
>
> Revelation 8:1–2

What is this silence in heaven? I believe it is the emptiness, the abyss, before God acts. There is nothing to do in heaven but to wait in silence until He is ready to move. Then the angels with the trumpets enter the stage and the action begins.

Facing the emptiness before God acts is the most difficult requirement of cooperating with Him. It involves learning to wait for God's time, then acting accordingly. A more familiar way of expressing this principle is to say that we must learn to wait on the Lord. If only we can do that, we are promised renewed strength and effectiveness:

> Even youths shall faint and be weary, and young men shall fall exhausted; but they who wait for the LORD shall renew their strength, they shall mount up with wings like eagles, they shall run and not be weary, they shall walk and not faint.
>
> Isaiah 40:30–31

178

I have always loved this verse! But to wait on the Lord is extremely difficult because it means we must face emptiness. We must put aside our own agendas, our own impatient activity, and give God the space to take the initiative and act, or to reveal to us how to act according to His purposes.

Willingness to face the abyss is the key to moving with God in power ministry.

Give God space? Is He not everywhere, filling all spaces as the omnipotent Lord, Creator of all things? Does He not, in Patrick Henry's words, "preside over the destinies of nations"?[1] God works independently and transcendent of us, of course, but here is a great mystery: He has included in His sovereignty and eternal decrees space for our prayers and obedience.

We see Him giving space to us in the mystic vision of Revelation. After the half-hour of silence, before the drama of God's action proceeds, this verse appears: "The smoke of the incense, together with the prayers of the saints, went up before God from the angel's hand" (Revelation 8:4, NIV). God stops the action to allow space for the prayers of the saints, which are then included in God's actions. This mutually given space, and our participation in God's actions, takes place because of the love that flows from the mutuality of our relationship. It is possible because we have been born again as sons and daughters who call Him, through Jesus, *Abba*.

Usually in worship, prayer, counseling, meetings or implementing our goals, we fill all the available space with talk or activity. We are terrified of empty spaces and we rush to fill them. Yet those spaces, when pregnant with the presence of the Holy Spirit, often become the times of God's miraculous activity.

Not Acting Until God Acts

The most common context in which we face emptiness is while we are doing the work of prayer.

I was leading a group of 140 people in a prayer event right after the Gulf War. We went from one topic to the next until we had finished praying through our list. The Holy Spirit was tangibly present but nothing was happening.

As the seconds turned to minutes, I fought the temptation to encourage everyone to sing a hymn or read some Scripture, just to fill the emptiness. As time wore on, people started to get restless. As the leader I was feeling like a fool. I considered dismissing the group and taking a break.

Deep inside, however, I knew God was getting ready to do something. It was not just the silence of emptiness but the silence of presence, the half hour of silence before God acted. How did I know? Because I had lived through this silence in the wilderness! There I had been reduced to stillness and had had my ambitions killed.

Although the silence in the prayer room was like facing an abyss, my wilderness training held and we waited. I even hushed several premature attempts to move into praise.

After what seemed an eternity (it was about thirty minutes), I was aware of the presence of the Holy Spirit moving in our midst. Along with this movement I received the gift of faith and sensed that God was about to act.

Then a man started to cry softly. I went up to him and asked, "What is it?"

He stood and said tearfully, "As we waited on the Lord, a great burden came on me for the Kurds."

As he spoke, the whole group was seized with a spirit of intercession for those people driven into the mountains by the Iraqi army. Children and the elderly were dying from hunger and cold as the world looked on without giving aid. For more than an hour and a half we prayed with great urgency for the plight of the Kurdish people. It was a remarkable season of prayer and apparently in the flow of God's purposes.

Three days later a massive international aid effort was initiated by the French government. Our participation in God's compassionate work would have been missed if we had filled up the space in our program with something other than God's plan.

There are times we must pray without words or actions and simply wait expectantly on the Lord. This form of prayer requires the extreme discipline of not acting until God acts.

Waiting for God's Leading

Another context in which we may face the silence of God is in seeking guidance as to what we are to do.

For years I knew I was called to the work of evangelism. For years I prayed, "Lord, show me how." Then, through the ministry of PRRMI, I launched an evangelism program called "Jesus Encounters." The vision that had been born—partly in prayer, partly in my haste just to do something—was to mobilize churches in a target area for evangelistic outreach in that area.

We publicized the program. We tried a prototype in a church in New York State that was already moving in the Holy Spirit. Then we held our first Jesus Encounter event. There was great blessing and some people came to Christ. But the spiritual warfare was intense. The pastors decided that the cost was too great, for them personally and for their congregations. They were not prepared to go forward with Jesus Encounters.

I gave up on the program in discouragement. Week after week I went up the mountain asking God for guidance about what expression PRRMI's work of evangelism was to take. All the while, urgency grew in me for the task.

All sorts of ideas came. I saw lots of opportunity but received no clear guidance. Once again I found my wilderness training paying off. I was impatient but willing to face the emptiness of waiting. I fought the temptation to let my own imagination create words of guidance or to invent a program.

This went on for three years. Then one Sunday, just before a PRRMI board meeting at a church in Montreat, North Carolina, I attended a prayer meeting held each Sunday in the pastor's study. Church members gathered to pray for the Sunday school teachers, for the children and for the worship service.

The prayer time was wonderful. The Holy Spirit was moving to guide the prayers. Then I felt the Spirit stirring in me, giving me the gift of faith. It came as a vague, inarticulate awareness and a deep, peaceful, joyful certainty that God was going to act that day. His silence in regard to PRRMI's involvement in evangelism was about to be broken.

Throughout the worship service later, I sensed an undercurrent of joy as the Holy Spirit moved. I found, to my surprise, that the "Stephen Ministers" were to be commissioned that morning after a year of training. The pastor, Richard White, explained that the Stephen Ministers, lay workers modeled after Stephen's practical ministry in the book of Acts, had been trained to assist him and the elders with the pastoral care ministry of the church.[2]

After the sermon Pastor White and the elders gathered around the Stephen Ministers and laid hands on them. That was when God spoke to me, as clearly as someone speaking audibly behind me. It was the same way I had heard Him speak on the mountain in Korea. The import of the words echoed through my being, although later I could not recall the actual audible voice.

Yes, He said, *Stephen Ministers are good. But what I also want in My churches are Philip Ministers—those who will assist the pastor and leaders with doing the work of Holy Spirit–empowered evangelism.*

This blew my mind. I really do not know what happened during the rest of the service because I was caught up in vision after vision of how laypersons could be equipped to do the work of evangelism. I saw churches growing, and laymen and women sharing their faith with their neighbors. I saw healing evangelism, friendship evangelism, all mingling as tributaries of the rushing river of the advancing Kingdom of God worldwide. Like a sculptor who has caught a revelatory glimpse of the living form to be liberated from cold stone, and then with sure purpose picks up the chisel, I scribbled the contours of the vision on the edges of my church bulletin.

When I got home, I did a check through the concordance on Philip, and found both Philips, the apostle and the evangelist, to be perfect models for Spirit-guided and Spirit-empowered evangelism. No wonder God wanted people walking with the Holy Spirit like these two Philips! They were the secret to the equipping of congregations to bring people to saving faith in Jesus Christ.

When I presented this vision to the board of PRRMI, there was an enthusiastic "Yes! This is from God! Go for it!"

So we are moving out in action, confident that this plan is consistent with God's heart. The name of the vision is "The Philip Endeavor." Our role now is risk-taking obedience. Having faced the emptiness and waited on the Lord for His vision and program, we are going boldly forward, trusting that His power and gifts will accompany our efforts and that it is not we but Jesus acting.[3]

What about You?

Where are you in waiting on the Lord? Can you do it? Or is your impatience driving you to create something from your own desires or imagination? There are times we must act and decide without clear guidance. We discussed this earlier in the section on "going fishing." Mostly, however, when we go fishing, we are acting on guidance we have already received.

Waiting on the Lord pushes us to a deeper level of engagement with God and usually takes place at the hinge points in our lives when we are moving to a new calling and new levels of intimacy with Him. To know when to wait and when to push forward is one of the great gifts of the wilderness experience.

Do not misunderstand. This waiting on the Lord, born of the wilderness experience, is not laid-back passivity. Rather, in Arnold Toynbee's words, it is the "repose of a locomotive standing in the station under steam pressure, with its movement continuing as a stationary throbbing while it waits for the moment to make a new leap forward."[4]

Waiting on the Lord is intense listening prayer with one's gifts sharpened and a will prepared for obedience. It is like the virgins awaiting the bridegroom with lamps prepared. When the Lord says, "Go," you are ready to go.

You may be waiting for the right person to marry, for the right job, for the right opportunity for ministry. You may be in transition, out of attending or serving one church but not yet with a clear call to another. You see many needs and opportunities, but none seems right and no door is clearly open. You may be facing emptiness as you strive in prayer for your children or for someone you love and nothing is happening; there are no answers. You may be facing a pastoral situation in which you have done all the listening you can, but still there is no healing. You may find yourself before the congregation leading worship, bulletin in hand, yet in your soul you experience the thrill of expectation that God is about to act.

All these are times for facing the emptiness. You must be prepared, but you cannot move until God moves. It is in times like this that the wilderness finds its purpose. Having fought the battle of opposing wills and died to yourself, you can quell the storms within that are calling for action and face the terror of the emptiness in which nothing is happening.[5]

When we give this space to God, we will be astonished at what He does! We will also find it true that "they who wait for the LORD shall renew their strength . . . they shall run and not be weary. . . ."

When we have been brought to this point—living in Jesus Christ, and Jesus living and acting in us—then the wilderness has accomplished its purpose. We shall with Jesus go out in the power of the Holy Spirit to share with Him in the advancement of His Kingdom. Then all the pain of dying will give way to joy. And then we will thank God that He loved us enough to send us into the wilderness. It is all for God's glory!

Questions for Reflection

1. What has God taught you through the wilderness about the necessity of prayer?
2. Have you made a commitment to "go up the mountain" as the Holy Spirit leads you?
3. What has God taught you about facing emptiness?
4. Which situation in your life right now will you select as an opportunity to practice waiting on the Lord?
5. How do you know when you have reached the goal of the wilderness training, which is not our acting, but Christ acting through us?

Notes

Chapter 2: The Purpose of the Wilderness

1. William Alexander Percy, "They Cast Their Nets," *The Hymnbook* (Richmond, Va.: Presbyterian Church [U.S.A.], 1955), p. xxx.

2. For descriptions of experiences of the gifts and power of the Holy Spirit, see *The Collapse of the Brass Heaven: Rebuilding Our Worldview to Embrace the Power of God* (Grand Rapids: Chosen, 1994) and *Receiving the Power: Preparing the Way for the Holy Spirit* by Zeb Bradford Long and Douglas McMurry (Chosen, 1996). In these two books Doug and I lay out an understanding of spiritual reality and the working of the Holy Spirit that is assumed in this book on the wilderness.

3. This allusion to smoldering embers most likely has its inspiration in John Calvin's *Institutes of the Christian Religion*. In the section "Believers Are Still Sinners," he writes: "In this matter all writers of sounder judgment agree that there remains in a regenerate man a smoldering cinder of evil, from which desires continually leap forth to allure and spur him to commit sin" *(Institutes of the Christian Religion,* transl. by Ford Lewis Battles, ed. by John T. McNeill [Philadelphia: Westminster, 1960], p. 602).

Chapter 4: The Silence of God

1. I was first awakened to the power and reality of the Holy Spirit while in Korea at Jesus Abbey, a charismatic Anglican intercessory prayer community directed by the Rev. Archer Torrey, the grandson of R. A. Torrey. I describe this experience in chapter 17; and in more detail, with a biblical understanding, in the book Douglas McMurry and I co-authored, *Receiving the Power: Preparing the Way for the Holy Spirit.*

2. John Bailie, *A Diary of Private Prayer* (New York: Charles Scribner's Sons, 1955), p. 105.

Chapter 5: The Wilderness: A Place of Conflict

1. For my understanding of this ambiguous dimension of the devil's nature, I am deeply indebted to the book *Unmasking the Powers: The Invisible Forces that Determine Human Existence* by Walter Wink (Minneapolis: Fortress, 1986).

2. C. S. Lewis, *The Screwtape Letters* (New York: Macmillan, 1948), p. 9.

Chapter 6: The Demonic: Working for Our Destruction

1. Calvin, *Institutes,* I, 14, 13, p. 173.

2. I say *usually* because there are times they do not leave. The reason is found not

in any deficiency in the authority of Christ, but in the fact that we have not dealt adequately with the grounds of their entry.

3. The demonic dimension in this woman was confirmed two years later when, during a conference, she started to manifest an evil spirit. This led to a three-week exorcism. The demons had entered her through severe hurt and occult activity. (In order to protect the identity of the people involved, I have made this story a composite of several similar experiences with fasting.)

Chapter 7: Meeting the Devil as God's Tester

1. Louis J. Puhl, *The Spiritual Exercises of St. Ignatius: Based on Studies in the Language of the Autograph* (Chicago: Loyola University Press, 1951), pp. 145–146.

2. Ibid., p. 146.

Chapter 8: Wilderness as the Place to Know Ourselves

1. Calvin, *Institutes,* pp. 35–37.

Chapter 9: Dying to Illusions

1. According to Louis J. Puhl, *The Spiritual Exercises of St. Ignatius: Based on Studies in the Language of the Autograph* (Chicago: Loyola University Press, 1951), p. 142, St. Ignatius defines *spiritual consolation* in Rule 3 of the "Rules for the Discernment of Spirits" as follows: "I call it consolation when an interior movement is aroused in the soul, by which it is inflamed with love of its Creator and Lord, and as a consequence can love no creature on the face of the earth for its own sake, but only in the Creator of them all. It is likewise consolation when one sheds tears that move one to the love of God, whether it be because of sorrow for sins, or because of the sufferings of Christ our Lord, or for any other reason that is immediately directed to the praise and service of God. Finally, I call consolation every increase of faith, hope, and love, and all interior joy that invites and attracts to what is heavenly, and to the salvation of one's soul, by filling it with peace and quiet in its Creator and Lord."

Chapter 12: Under Judgment, Under Grace

1. Puhl, *Spiritual Exercises,* p. 29.

Chapter 15: God as Our Healer

1. A term from Charles Willams' book *The Descent of the Dove: A Short History of the Holy Spirit in the Church* (Grand Rapids: Eerdmans, 1939).

2. Many people have asked, "How do you manage even writing this book?" First, I have a wonderful wife who was an English major. I also have an excellent editor, a competent secretarial staff and a high-speed laptop computer that can spell quite well! God did, however, heal me of my dyslexia enough to learn to speak Chinese and to begin learning Portuguese.

Chapter 16: Called into God's Service

1. Calvin, *Institutes,* III, VII, 2, p. 690.

188

2. Oswald Chambers, *My Utmost for His Highest* (New York: Dodd, Mead, 1935), p. 24.

Chapter 17: Out of the Wilderness into New Empowerment

1. I know this is, as I said in the introduction, a controversial term. I believe the biblical understanding of the phrase *baptism with the Holy Spirit* is "the appropriation in faith of the empowering dimension of the Holy Spirit's work." One can use other biblical terms as well, such as *being filled with the Holy Spirit, the Holy Spirit upon, receiving the Holy Spirit* and *the gifts of the Holy Spirit.* All have to do with the "Spirit upon for power," and reflect an operation of the Holy Spirit distinct from the work of sanctification and salvation. For a more complete discussion of the power dimension of the Holy Spirit's work, please see my book co-authored with Douglas McMurry, *Receiving the Power: Preparing the Way for the Holy Spirit.* Some of the experiences given in this book are written up more completely in that one. Also, the Dunamis Project teaching manual of Presbyterian and Reformed Renewal Ministries International, *Gateways to Empowered Ministry: The Person and Work of the Holy Spirit* (Black Mountain, N.C.: PRRMI, 1997), provides a biblical and Reformed framework for understanding the empowering work of the Holy Spirit.

2. This story was told originally in a book by Zeb Bradford Long and Douglas McMurry, *Gateways to Empowered Ministry: The Person and Work of the Holy Spirit,* pp. 265–266.

Chapter 18: Beyond Wilderness: Walking with Jesus in Intimacy and Fruitfulness

1. From Patrick Henry's "Give me liberty or give me death" speech to the Virginia Convention, Richmond, Va., March 23, 1775. Also from Isaiah 40:23: "He brings princes to naught and reduces the rulers of this world to nothing" (NIV).

2. The Stephen Ministries is a nonprofit, religious and educational organization developed to provide a lay caring ministry within the Church. It was developed by Kenneth C. Haugk in the 1970s and is based in St. Louis, Missouri.

3. I put myself at some risk for including the vision for "The Philip Endeavor" in this book. The process of receiving this vision was taking place as I was writing the last chapter, so it has not yet been fully confirmed from the Lord. The final test will be when it really happens and evangelism starts to take place in the churches. The risk is that I may not have heard clearly from the Lord, or that sin and disobedience on someone's part will block the fulfillment of the vision.

4. Arnold J. Toynbee, *A Study of History* (New York: Oxford University Press, 1947), p. 212.

5. This brings us to the concept of *kairos* moments—occasions when the Holy Spirit is ready to act in a person, place or situation. *Kairos* time is the Greek concept of time that is fulfilled, as distinct from chronological time like seconds, minutes, hours and days. This concept is elaborated on in the section "Principles of Power Ministry" in the Dunamis manual, *In the Spirit's Power: Growing in the Gifts of the Holy Spirit* (Black Mountain, N.C.: PRRMI, 1998).

Bibliography

Bailie, John. *A Diary of Private Prayer.* New York: Charles Scribner's Sons, 1955.

Calvin, John. *Institutes of the Christian Religion.* Transl. by Ford Lewis Battles. Ed. by John T. McNeill. Philadelphia: Westminster, 1975.

Lewis, C. S. *The Screwtape Letters.* New York: Macmillan, 1948.

Long, Zeb Bradford and Douglas McMurry. *The Collapse of the Brass Heaven: Rebuilding Our Worldview to Embrace the Power of God.* Grand Rapids: Chosen, 1994.

——————. *Receiving the Power: Preparing the Way for the Holy Spirit.* Grand Rapids: Chosen, 1996.

Percy, William Alexander. "They Cast Their Nets." *The Hymnbook.* Richmond, Va.: Presbyterian Church (USA), 1955.

Puhl, Louis J. *The Spirtual Exercises of St. Ignatius: Based on Studies in the Language of the Autograph.* Chicago: Loyola University Press, 1951.

Toynbee, Arnold J. *A Study of History.* New York: Oxford University Press, 1947.

Williams, Charles. *The Descent of the Dove: A Short History of the Holy Spirit in the Church.* Grand Rapids: Eerdmans, 1939.

Wink, Walter. *Unmasking the Powers: The Invisible Forces that Determine Human Existence.* Minneapolis: Fortress, 1986.

Zeb Bradford Long, ordained in the Presbyterian Church (U.S.A.), has a D.Min. from Union Theological Seminary in Richmond, Virginia.

In 1980 Dr. Long and his wife, the Rev. Laura Long, were appointed by the Presbyterian Church as evangelists/educational missionaries to Taiwan (the Republic of China). While there Dr. Long served as founder and director of the Presbyterian Lay Training Center and vice president of the Presbyterian Bible College. He also served on various committees of the Taiwan Presbyterian Church General Assembly and, during his last year there, as chairman of the PCUSA Taiwan Mission.

In 1990 Dr. Long joined Presbyterian and Reformed Renewal Ministries as executive director. His fourfold vision for PRRMI includes prayer, leadership development, congregational renewal and mission outreach. He has a deep desire to see churches of the Reformed tradition moving in the gifts and power of the Holy Spirit.

Dr. Long resides with his wife and three children, Elizabeth, Rebecca and Stephen, in Black Mountain, North Carolina.

For more information, write to

Presbyterian & Reformed
Renewal Ministries International
P.O. Box 429
Black Mountain, NC 28711-0429

The address for PRRMI's website is:

www.prrmi.org